One Frenchman, Four Revolutions

General Ferrand and the Peoples of the Caribbean

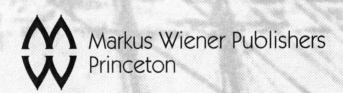

Markus Wiener Publishers
Princeton

One Frenchman, Four Revolutions

FERNANDO PICÓ

For information, write to:
Markus Wiener Publishers
231 Nassau Street, Princeton, NJ 08542
www.markuswiener.com

Library of Congress Cataloging-in-Publication Data
Picó, Fernando.
    One Frenchman, four revolutions : general Ferrand and the peoples of
the Caribbean / Fernando Picó.
        p. cm.
    Includes bibliographical references.
    ISBN 978-1-55876-539-9 (hc. : alk. paper)
    ISBN 978-1-55876-540-5 (pbk. : alk. paper)
    1. Ferrand, Marie-Louis, 1758-1808. 2. Hispaniola—History.
    3. Haiti—History—Revolution, 1791-1804. 4. Dominican Republic—
    History—To 1844. 5. French—Dominican Republic— History—
    19th century. 6. Generals—France—Biography. I. Title.
        F1923.F47P53 2011
        355.0092--dc22
        [B]
                                        2011010565

Markus Wiener Publishers books are printed in the United States
of America on acid-free paper and meet the guidelines for permanence
and durability of the Committee on Production Guidelines for Book
Longevity of the Council on Library Resources.

Contents

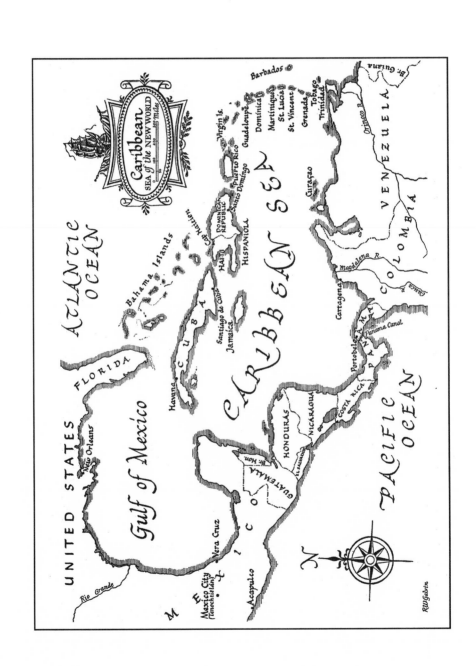

Preface

On November 7, 1808, defeated, depressed, and practically alone, General Marie-Louis Ferrand took out his pistol and committed suicide. The fifty-year-old captain general of Santo Domingo and, since December 1803, commander in chief of the occupying French troops had just lost the military encounter that in the Dominican Republic is celebrated as the Battle of Palo Hincado. For someone who had prevailed over so many challenges, it was an unexpected end. Throughout his long military career, Ferrand had confronted a number of menaces that threatened to erase the rationality with which he pretended to rule his life. At each turning point, he had been successful in overcoming adversity. But on this last occasion, he was unable to forestall defeat, and his answer was to take his own life.

This book examines General Ferrand's administration of Santo Domingo between 1803 and 1808 in the light of the revolutionary world in which his military career developed. There is a tendency either to ignore the impact of the Atlantic Revolution on the Caribbean islands or to treat each island or group of islands in isolation from the rest. In the case of Santo Domingo, national and racial issues tend to blur some aspects of the French and Haitian interventions in Dominican society. Ferrand's administration has been seen primarily within those limits. Although much more remains to be done on the subject, this book seeks to point out interesting lines of research that may widen our understanding of French policies in the Caribbean and their impact on island societies.

This is a book about the world in which Ferrand thrived and in which he ultimately lost his life. He was one among thousands of French actors in the American Revolutionary War. He served in the French army before and during the French Revolution. He volunteered to serve in Saint-Domingue when Napoleon decided to retake control of the French colony. When the rebelling slaves repulsed the French and proclaimed the independence of Haiti, Ferrand took com-

mand of the remaining French forces and for five years kept the eastern part of Hispaniola for France. The last revolution he witnessed was
the one staged by Dominicans against himself and the French regime
in Santo Domingo.

Though this book is not a biography of Ferrand, his figure serves as
the link between the four revolutions through which he lived. As
such, it visualizes the five decades of revolutions between 1775 and
1825 as a unit, rather than as separate strands as the revolutions span-
ning those decades are usually studied and taught. One sees the continuum of the four revolutions throughout the career of one man,
and thus, in the tradition of historians Jacques Godechot and Robert
Palmer, one envisages the revolutionary world of that period as a unit.

In the course of my research on General Ferrand and his world, I
have received welcome help from different institutions and persons.
At the Archivo General de Puerto Rico, José Flores and his staff have
been ever ready to facilitate ongoing research. At the General Library
at the University of Puerto Rico, Río Piedras campus, I would like to
acknowledge the many kindnesses extended at the Colección
Puertorriqueña, the Colección Josefina Fulladosa del Toro, and the
Biblioteca del Caribe. The Centro de Investigaciones Históricas at the
Humanities College of the same campus has been a second home, for
which I am grateful to its director, Lolita Luque, and to Josué
Caamaño, Miriam Lugo, and Magaly Cintrón. This book owes much
to the assistance received in the summer of 2008 at the Archives
Nationales in Paris and the Manuscript Collection of the Bibliotheque
Nationale.

My colleagues in the Humanities, Social Sciences, and General
Studies colleges at the University of Puerto Rico were of great assistance throughout. I am grateful to the committee that recommended
me for the Eugenio María de Hostos chair for the year 2007–2008,
which made possible my research in France in the summer of 2008.
Finally, I would like to express my gratitude to Markus Wiener and to
Molan Goldstein for their editorial care with the manuscript of this
book.

I dedicate this book to my former classmates at Saint Andrew on
Hudson between 1959 and 1963, both to those who stayed in the
Jesuit Order and to those who chose other paths to greater glory.

The Atlantic Revolution and Its Caribbean Scenarios

Naval battle in the Caribbean, eighteenth century.

In the 1960s, Jacques Godechot and Robert Palmer popularized the notion of an Atlantic or Democratic Revolution that had encompassed both sides of the Atlantic world.[1] Starting with the city-state of Geneva in 1765, and extending to thirteen of the seventeen British North American colonies in the 1770s,[2] a series of revolutionary movements in the 1780s and 1790s had gone on to sweep the ancien régimes from the Low Countries, France, Italy, and many other parts of Europe. Although Godechot placed more stress on the socioeconomic factors and Palmer on the ideological and political motifs, they both advanced the notion that the institutions by which the North Atlantic societies had been governed were challenged and discarded as insufficient to meet the challenges of expanding commerce, burgeoning populations, and an increasingly educated public. In the

1

1990s, Lester Langley extended this analysis to other parts of the New World and stressed the continuity between the first wave of revolutions and the subsequent disruptions of the established order in Saint-Domingue and the Spanish Main.[3]

Considerations on the Atlantic Revolution have tended to represent the Caribbean societies as marginal to the general revolutionary movement and, with the exception of Haiti, as largely passive and unconcerned with the ideas and the debates that agitated the North Atlantic. At best, the Caribbean Sea was one of the settings in which the Old World powers clashed in their efforts to promote or contain the revolutionary tides. Nothing of consequence happening in the islands greatly mattered on either side of the Atlantic in the general scheme of things.

Unconsciously, such attitudes reflect the notion that the enslaved and peasant populations of the Caribbean were uninformed and necessarily alienated from the great currents of their day. Political conscience has been constructed as a by-product of literacy.[4] Surely current discussions on the shortcomings of the idealized Enlightenment have dented the easy assumptions that had been made about popular cultures, subordinates' political awareness, and the vitality of traditional political discourses.

To envisage the Caribbean as an important theater of the Atlantic Revolution, one must remember that it was the vigorous trade in Caribbean commodities that had animated the English and French ports, created the great fortunes on which the political careers of so many European (and North American) statesmen rested, and sharpened the naval rivalry between Great Britain and France. In the second half of the eighteenth century, the fate of the rich colonies of Saint-Domingue, Cuba, Jamaica, and Barbados weighed more on the deliberations of European cabinets than did the pamphlets of Boston and Philadelphia.

The Caribbean at the Period
of the Atlantic Revolution

Successive waves agitated the Caribbean at this time: the American, French, and Haitian revolutions; the wars for Hispano-American independence; and the British and French slave emancipation movements. Different imaginaries, linked by common references, caught the attention of the Caribbean islands in the period between the American Revolution and the emancipation of the slaves in the British-ruled islands. The libertarian currents that lit up Haiti in the 1790s were sparked by the traditions of individual acts of resistance and of maroon communities as well as by the revolutionary slogans coming in from France. The "Fear of Haiti" that propagated itself among the dominant sectors of society in the rest of the Caribbean both stimulated and challenged the anti-slavery currents fostered by either enlightened thought or the fervors of religious renewal. Sparks from the North Atlantic revolutions not only took hold on the Spanish American continental lands but also in the Caribbean islands.

In this period, the Caribbean societies experimented with the most important institutional changes that took place between the age of the original European settlements and the granting of independence in the second half of the twentieth century. Part of the reason for these changes arose from the fact that the Caribbean was then the focus of European rivalries and intrigues. With its territories criss-crossed by political agents from both the north and the south, its commercial routes harassed by privateers from different jurisdictions, and its economies tied up by the credit extension practices of the great commercial houses of the North Atlantic, the Caribbean world evoked the most bizarre enterprises and the most emblematic projects of the age.

After the 1830s, the Europeans' interest was displaced. The Spanish American societies concentrated on their own national agendas, and the Caribbean islands remained as a secondary theater for the representatives of the new industrial and economic world order. Only Cuba occasionally aroused some interest, in the 1890s and again in the 1960s. The Caribbean islands, which were reportedly unhealthy for Europeans in the initial decades of the nineteenth century, became by the beginning of the twenty-first century the paradise of the fantasies and the caprices of North Atlantic people. Only the sand, the sun, the music, and the casinos came to be of interest to the northerners, and the peoples of the Caribbean had to migrate or become taxi drivers or renters of boats to the lords of the euro and the dollar.

One interesting aspect of studying the revolutionary decades in the Caribbean is to observe the degree of interrelationship among the islands, perhaps greater then than in the rest of the nineteenth century. The British seemed to own the Caribbean, a lake patrolled by the Royal Navy for the convenience of the merchants of London, Liverpool, and Bristol. The French dreamed of recovering Saint-Domingue, and once they became convinced of the futility of that enterprise, they searched for an adequate substitute. The Spanish clung to their two remaining islands, Cuba and Puerto Rico, which they came to value after the loss of their continental empire. But while the ruling powers of the Caribbean composed their aspirations, what did the inhabitants of the islands do?

Alternative Visions of the Caribbean

To some historians, the Caribbean islands were the source of funding, provisioning and refuge for mainland revolutionaries from Venezuela and, to a lesser degree, from Mexico. Haiti acquired a centrality in revolutionary narratives, which it then ironically lost when the independences obtained with its support consolidated. Of analogous importance were Curaçao and Saint Thomas. Venezuelan historiography has persistently attributed to Haiti's influence the antislavery movement of the 1790s. It has also highlighted the primordial importance of financing obtained in Curaçao, and the crucial role of Saint Thomas as a source of military supplies. Simón Bolívar's travels through Curaçao, Jamaica, and Haiti constituted an important part of the epic narrative attached to the figure of "the Liberator."

But if the Caribbean islands have figured prominently in the narratives of the Spanish American revolutions, they are also mentioned in accounts of the efforts to smother the revolutions. As supply depots for the monarchical troops, Cuba and Puerto Rico played a part in the respective revolutions of New Spain and Venezuela. They also served as places of asylum for the pro-monarchical refugees.

Historians have also remarked on the Caribbean's function as a location for the power plays of the navies of Great Britain, France, and the United States. These countries were eager to affirm their authority, maintain a check on privateers' activities, and forestall adventurers' coups that went against their interests.

These stories are interesting, but they should not monopolize our attention. It would be more useful to know, compare, and ponder the experiences of Caribbean peoples at a period in which the Caribbean was a battlefield for the European powers. Insular inhabitants did not have the power to control events in their immediate zone, but they did have the initiative to shape their lives in the midst of those events.

Narratives about subalterns may fasten on their aspirations to power, but we must not forget that day-to-day concerns absorb most of their energies. What in the long run reflects the subalterns' daily struggles and engagements more than the imprint of the dominant sectors' projects? That is why the history of the Caribbean islands in this period should be studied not only from the viewpoint of the rulers but also from the agency of the islanders themselves.

The Caribbean Islands in the Atlantic Revolutionary Period

We may imagine the Caribbean islands at that time as appearing identical to those of our own day, but those lands, shaped by movements of the earth more than fifty million years ago, have not ceased changing. Earthquakes, hurricanes, volcanoes, droughts, winds, and rains have molded the mountains, coastlines, and river courses. But above all, human agency has upset the ancient ecological balances.

The deforestation of most islands, the damming up of rivers, the pro-
liferation of houses and roads, the mutilation of reefs, the appropriation of swamps and wetlands, the erosion and the leveling of hills,
the progressive extinction of native fauna and flora have altered the
islands so that they appear quite different than they did to navigators
in the time of Napoleon.

The great hurricane of 1780 was still alive in the memory of many
islanders,[5] as was the earthquakes of 1787. In the first third of the
nineteenth century, the numerous hurricanes were disastrous for
economies highly dependent on agriculture and cattle raising. A hurricane that struck Puerto Rico on September 11, 1806, moved Toribio
de Montes, the Spanish governor, to write in a circular letter issued
two days afterward:

> The disaster that this capital has experienced the day before yes-
> terday, on account of a furious hurricane which in three and a
> half hours has made visible the nefarious destruction of which
> the air agitated on all sides in succession is capable, makes me
> fear the same evils throughout the extension of the island, and
> also in the neighboring ones.[6]

A year later, Montes wrote to the local authorities that a recent
storm had rendered the roads useless, and he urged them to form
local groups to deliberate on their early repair. He gave them until
November to carry out the labors.[7]

That same hurricane had struck the island of Dominica. The course
of the Roseau River was changed and the capital of the island was
flooded. One hundred and thirty-one people died. In July and August
of 1813, two hurricanes destroyed the seat of government and
prompted a chronicler to affirm: "I have never witnessed such havoc
and destruction in so small a compass and how to convey the sad
intelligence I am really at a loss." There was another hurricane in July
1823, but the memorable one was the Great Hurricane of 1834, in
which 200 people died.[8]

Volcanoes and earthquakes also marked life in Caribbean societies.
In Guadeloupe there was a volcanic explosion in 1788 and another

one in 1799.[9] The famous Maundy Thursday earthquake that terrorized the residents of Caracas may have been linked to an explosion of the Soufrière volcano, which spilled lava over the island of Saint Vincent in 1812.[10]

But in those islands where sugarcane had become the principal crop, recurring droughts constituted the greatest worry. With increasing frequency, the droughts entered into the calculations of the London merchants, the planters, and the administrators. In some islands, like Barbados, the soils had lost their primitive fertility at a pace that augured ill for the stability of sugar production. Already in the 1780s, investors from the Bordelais were conscious of the alternation of droughts and floods in the Artibonite Plain in Saint-Domingue.[11] In 1796 the drought in Jamaica was so severe that it was still being recalled thirty-five years later.[12] The drought of 1796 in Santo Domingo delayed the departure of some migrants from Santiago, to whom money was owed.[13] What made the undeveloped islands attractive to sugar planters was the humidity retained by their forests and the fertility of their unexploited soils.

Unity and Diversity of the Caribbean Islands

Struck by the same natural phenomena, linked by the sea, the islanders shared some features and differed in other regards. In part the similarities and the differences resulted from the European and African origins of its population and of the remnants of indigenous populations that, in varying proportions, survived on some of the islands. But much may also arise from the size, topography, population density, and peculiar history of each island, along with its location on the Caribbean map, to which side of the winds, how close it was to the continent, and what kinds of soil covered the surface. The island of Curaçao, for instance, which was not endowed with fertile soils or sufficient rainfall, derived from its proximity to the coast of Venezuela its crucial role in trade and banking.[14]

Population and Economy

The population explosion that took place in the eighteenth century had an impact on Caribbean demographics. Almost all the islands experienced the greatest population growth in their history, especially in regard to the people of African origin. Antigua, for instance, had 2,892 white inhabitants in 1707 and only 1,890 in 1821, but it counted 12,892 slaves in 1707 and 31,964 in 1821.[15]

But while the proportion of the population of African origins grew more rapidly than that of European descent in the English- and French-speaking Caribbean, the rest of the Caribbean had other experiences. Until 1760, Cuba had Spanish and African immigration in stable proportions, but after 1760 there began the massive influx of slaves that reconfigured the profile of the Cuban population. By 1817, the Cuban census reported 257,380 whites, 115,691 free people of color, and 199,219 slaves, for a total population of 572,363 persons.[16] In Hispaniola, while the African component of the population increased more sharply than the European component on the French side, the Spanish side maintained the proportion of its European and African components. In Puerto Rico, the African population did not begin to grow rapidly until 1784, with the liberalization of licenses for slave importations, but it was the free population of color that held the highest proportion of the total population. Curaçao had a heavy proportion of residents of European descent, especially Jews, in a context in which trade and not agriculture was the dominant economic activity. Its population of African descent did not experience remarkable increase. In the Danish Virgin Islands, while the African population in Sainte Croix grew rapidly in the nineteenth century, it was not as well sustained in Saint Thomas. On the Swedish island of Saint Bartholomew, after the French ceded the island to Sweden in the 1780s, the pattern of small farms with few slaves was kept.[17] Here trade and some crafts accounted for a fair share of economic activity.

Although in this period in the English- and French-speaking Caribbean, the black slave population prevailed, there were important differences in the demographic patterns of the islands. There was a marked contrast between Barbados, where the births of children of slave mothers exceeded the deaths of slaves,[18] and Jamaica, where it seemed crucial to keep up slave labor by means of the continuous introduction of Africans. In Puerto Rico, marriages between slaves and free people in the eighteenth century made the distinction less decisive, but in the nineteenth century the number of church marriages by slaves diminished and the distinction between the free people of color and slaves grew. The proportion of the free people of color was highest in Puerto Rico. In the French-ruled Caribbean, it was significantly higher than in the English-ruled islands.

Complementary Economies

In the Spanish-ruled islands, the original settlements grew around the exploitation of gold. Once gold became scarce, cattle were raised in support of the conquering expeditions on the Continent, and sugarcane, ginger, tobacco and other crops were planted for the official market in Seville. French and English settlements were from the very beginning oriented toward commercial agriculture. First tobacco was tried, then sugarcane. The Dutch saw the islands they occupied as depots for American merchandise to send to Europe and of European goods to be distributed in the New World. Although the Danish-ruled islands tried their hand with sugarcane growing, the Dutch used Saint Thomas throughout the eighteenth century to foster their own trade, without the inconvenience caused by the intervention of the United Provinces in European wars.[19]

The prosperity of the English- and French-ruled islands stimulated, too, the development of eastern Cuba, Santo Domingo, and Puerto Rico. With the exception of Havana, favored as the departure point for the Spanish fleet in its annual return trip to Seville, the rest of Cuba had little participation in official Spanish trade. But given the degree to which the English and French islands devoted their lands to cash crops for European markets, they had less land available for the raising of cattle, the cultivation of subsistence crops, and the supply of lumber for construction and other uses. The needs of these islands were complementary with those of the Spanish. Very early in the seventeenth century, the Dutch had detected in the Spanish islands avidity for European goods. The English and the French, together with the Dutch, learned smuggling skills. In this way, the Spanish islanders supplied the cattle, vegetables, and wood to the other islands in exchange for textiles, tools, and other goods that Spanish official trade did not bring to them.

The complementary character of the island economies was periodically put on trial on account of European wars. To the exasperation of the rulers, the inhabitants of eastern Cuba, Santo Domingo, and Puerto Rico continued to supply the other Europeans with the basic necessities in spite of the hostile activities of the metropolitan powers.

Conflicts, Solidarities, and Diversity of Social Controls

The different economies fostered alternative forms of social organization. In some areas, large producers prevailed, with a concentration of slave labor. In others areas, small and middling farmers with few or no slaves prevailed, relying on family labor and strong network of blood ties and godparent links throughout the land they occupied.

The prevalence of slavery in most Caribbean societies implied a conflictive character for social relations.[20] On some islands, like Barbuda, the starkly punitive character of penalties for slave transgressions kept society in a constant state of tension. Fear of slave rebellions is reflected in the penal codes of the eighteenth century. On the other hand, slaves' flights offered different possibilities, depending on the island.[21] In Jamaica, the maroon communities of the Blue Hills forced the authorities to ally with the former slaves.[22] In Cuba, the Sierra Maestra allowed for the survival of communities of fugitive slaves, but the mountains also spurred the use of bounty hunters who tracked fugitives to their hideouts.[23] For the slaves in Saint-Domingue, the sparse population in the Spanish part of the island offered a sure refuge for the fugitives. Runaways from the English and Dutch Caribbean islands found official sanctuary in

Puerto Rico, where they were guaranteed freedom in exchange for an oath of fidelity to the king of Spain and the adoption of the Catholic faith. In wartime, slaves from Martinique and Guadeloupe found shelter in Dominica, once this island passed under English dominion. Slaves fleeing Antigua sought sanctuary in Saint Eustatius or Guadeloupe.[24] Saint Vincent, the last major island to be occupied, had given refuge to fugitive slaves among the Caribs in the early decades of the eighteenth century. Slaves on the southern islands sought asylum on the continent.

In this fashion, insular tensions from slave resistance found a release in flight to other territories. The support and assistance that was illegal if offered to fugitives from local bondage could be proffered to the slave running away from the rivals' island.

Differences between slaves and free people were not the only cause of social conflict. Racial differences resulted in laws that discriminated against people of color and impeded their access to public office, church ministry, and military service. Even schooling became difficult for people of color on some islands.

On the more prosperous islands, there were notable differences between rich and poor white persons. In Saint-Domingue, these conflicts divided society so markedly that the coming of the French Revolution and its conflicts constituted the last stage of a long history of differences that precipitated the loss of French dominion over that rich colony.[25]

The number of poor whites tended to dwindle in the English Caribbean, but there was an elaborate framework of administrators, overseers, agents, and artisans where those who resented economic differences could find a niche.

Population Shifts

In the latter decades of the eighteenth century, immigrants arrived in the Caribbean from Africa and Europe, but there were also displacements and population shifts within the Caribbean. The British finally moved out the indigenous people from Saint Vincent and deported them to the Caribbean shores of the island of Rattan near the coast of Honduras.[26] From there they moved to Honduras, where their descendants, the *garifonas,* still live and retain their ancestral language. The British occupation of several French islands also resulted in the displacement of some indigenous population, for instance, in Dominica, some of whose inhabitants migrated to Trinidad. Later, the British occupation of Trinidad in 1797 displaced some Spaniards from the island. The cession of Spanish Santo Domingo to France under the Treaty of Basel of 1795 initiated the movement of its population to the neighboring islands of Cuba and Puerto Rico. But it was above all the Haitian Revolution that resulted in the greatest displacement of persons.

Political Institutions

The variety of governmental arrangements that prevailed in the Caribbean until the early nineteenth century is noteworthy. Until 1791, Curaçao was ruled by the West Indies Company, with its headquarters in Amsterdam.[27] Since 1680, Barbuda was the possession of one family, the Codringtons, who held the island as a fief from the Crown of England.[28] Some of the British islands had deliberative bodies, while the more recent acquisitions did not.[29] After 1797, Trinidad retained under British rule its *cabildo.* Captains general governed the Spanish islands, but the *audiencia,* or appeals court, had its seat in Santo Domingo, until it moved to Puerto Principe (Camaguey) in Cuba after the French occupied the Spanish part of Hispaniola.[30]

Religious Movements

The Pietist movements that arose in the center of Europe at the end of the seventeenth century influenced the religious revival in England at the beginning of the eighteenth.[31] From there, different currents of Christian reaffirmation, centered on personal experiences of conversion, reached the United States and the Caribbean. Of greatest impact was the Methodism preached by John Wesley.

An aspect of primary importance in the diffusion of Methodism in the Caribbean was the preaching of the Gospel to the slaves. Generally, in the English-speaking Caribbean, the agents and administrators who oversaw the sugarcane plantations did not have in their agenda the introduction of African slaves to the religious practices of the Church of England. Methodists put particular attention on reaching the slaves. In the first years of their missionary activity, this commitment came into conflict with the dominant sectors in the islands and with the colonial councils.

The first Methodist missionaries arrived in Saint Vincent in January 1787. They were given permission to preach on the court's premises, but they ran into conflict with the Assembly. This body passed a resolution prohibiting future missionaries from preaching. The Methodists had to appeal to their contacts in the British Parliament to have the Crown invalidate the decree.[32]

In Dominica, although there were missionaries since 1787, a minister was expelled from the island in 1796 for having asked to be excused from military exercises on Sundays:

> The president, after he had heard the petition, told him that he had been informed he was a very suspicious character, who disseminated pernicious doctrines among the slaves and instead of being exempted from military duty, he would compel him to quit the island, and gave him an order accordingly, with which order he was obliged to comply to avoid imprisonment.[33]

The Barbadian experience was somewhat more complex. According to Hilary Beckles, in the eighteenth century, the Methodists and the Moravians challenged the received notion that the effect of Christianizing the slaves would be to make them more resistant to their enslavement. The Methodists taught slave children to read and write, in opposition to the Anglican tenet that slave literacy was dangerous. In 1823, a Methodist chapel was destroyed by white members of a community who rejected an anti-slavery pamphlet published by its minister. But there was an Anglican priest, W.

M. Harte, who was taken to court for "inculcating doctrines" of racial equality. Accused of committing a misdemeanor, he was found guilty and was fined one shilling. He appealed and King George IV remitted the fine.[34]

In the Danish Virgin Islands, the religious revival came a little later from Europe, but it also led to the evangelization of the slave population.[35] Ministry to the population of African origin in the French Caribbean islands has not been as well studied, but Philippe Delisle has argued that, at least for Martinique, parish priests had little contact with the slave population in the plantations, but they did minister to the free colored population in their parishes.[36]

In the Hispanic Caribbean, the bishops directed that slaves be baptized, be married canonically, and be present at the Eucharist on Sundays and feast days. Their influence was more telling in the eighteenth century than in the nineteenth.[37]

Religious tolerance accorded to the Jews in Amsterdam was extended to the Dutch settlements in the Caribbean. The oldest synagogue in the New World is in Curaçao.[38]

Languages and Cultures

English, Spanish, and French were then the languages most spoken in the Caribbean, but they were not the only ones. Not only had aboriginal languages survived in some of the islands, but also, on account of the hybrid uses of the European and African languages there, new forms of speech arose. The Dutch did not impose their tongue, but the Papiamento dialect that arose in Curaçao and Aruba bore witness to the cultural encounters in which those islands abounded. Papiamento has been described as a mixture of Portuguese, Dutch, English, Spanish, French, and African languages.[39] In Curaçao's schools, however, French was taught in preference to any other language in the first decades of the nineteenth century.

Another Dutch island, Saint Eustatius, developed its own version of English. Since it was a center of commerce with the British-ruled islands, English became the language of trade, but it evolved its own grammar.[40]

In Saint Lucia, the British tried to replace French as the language of the courts, but it took them half a century to achieve it.[41] Although a majority of the rural population spoke Creole, French has ever been an official language there.

The predominant culture on each island was oral. Formal schooling developed slowly. The British Caribbean was first to develop a school system, but on some of the islands, like Saint Kitts, free people of color were excluded from the schools as late as 1830.[42] The fact that the free people of color in Saint Kitts helped pay for its public school system provided a legal basis for equality in schooling.

In Curaçao, the Jews maintained their own schools, and gave preference to the teaching of languages.[43] They also provided early mentions of libraries. Mordechai de Jeudah, Sr., left a thousand books in several languages when he died in 1756. Doctor Benjamin de Solas brought nine boxes of books from Holland, which were mentioned after his death in 1817. In 1821, Obadia de Costa offered for sale a collection of books in English. In 1833, Haim Abinum de Lima left at his death 391 books, and Abraham H. de Meza left 294 books when he died in 1846.[44] The numbers may seem slight by today's standards, but they offer a marked contrast to the small number of books mentioned in the inventories of deceased persons' goods in the Spanish Caribbean.

CHAPTER 2

The Atlantic Revolution in Its Caribbean Context

Naval battle in New Orleans during the American Revolution.

The eighteenth-century revolutions were not only about government or finances and taxes. They were also, as Christopher Grasso has written, about who could address the general public, on which matters, and on which occasions.[1] Equality not only meant equality before the law and equal access to the courts. Because the North American Revolution triumphed in the initial stages of the Atlantic Revolution, not all the implications of the revolutionary ideas in the air were worked out by the time the French Revolution, in the name of human rights, attempted the eradication of hierarchies and rank. That led, in turn, to the abolition of slavery in the French colonies, but that meant a challenge to absolute property rights as well. Equal opportunity and economic equality should have been the result, but then, commencing with Napoleon's regime in France, reaction set in and the Atlantic Revolution began to be phased out.

17

The North American Prequel

The American Revolution had begun as a family quarrel among British subjects. The British Parliament wanted to shift to the American colonies some of the financial burden that the French and Indian War (called in Europe the Seven Years' War) had imposed on the British treasury. Since the removal of the French garrisons north and west of the continental colonies benefited the Americans, what could be more logical than having the colonies assume part of the ensuing costs of the war? Thus thought the members of the British ruling elite. Besides, it was generally known that Americans eluded paying duties on many of the trade goods brought from the West Indies. Even such a respectable merchant as John Hancock, of Boston, habitually paid only a fraction of the duties for the molasses, rum, sugar, and other goods brought from the Caribbean.[2]

The bungling attempts of the British Parliament to meet the grievances of the American colonists and, at the same time, to penalize their resistance against the Stamp Act of 1765 has been told many times. Once lobbying in London, the traditional recourse of the American elites, had ceased to be useful, the leading voices in the colonies, particularly in Massachusetts and Pennsylvania, had organized committees to deliberate and represent the colonists' grievances. They also began to turn the colonial militias to their own agenda, and to undermine the colonial governors' efforts to halt the deterioration of the inherited political fabric.

It is not necessary to recount here the development of the Continental Congress, the first armed encounters with the British in Massachusetts, the radicalization of the movement, and the declaration of independence of the colonies in 1776. But for the Caribbean societies, the North American colonists' search for support meant that a fair number of newspapers, pamphlets, and other publications found their way to the islands, mixed with the cargoes of pine, turpentine, flour, and tools. There were echoes of the North American grievances in some of the island councils' deliberations, but after all, they had had their own share of complaints and confrontations with the British Parliament, which wanted the islands to help maintain the British fleet that defended their interests. The islands, however, had one advantage. Many of the absentee plantation owners lived in England, where they not only lobbied actively in behalf of their own interests, but as Sir Lewis Namier showed, they also called the votes of a significant number of the members of Parliament.[3]

No account of the American War of Independence can bypass the crucial contribution to the success of the rebel cause made by the entry of France, Spain, and the United Provinces of the Netherlands on the side of the revolutionaries. These alliances were the fruit of intense lobbying.[4] The financial sacrifices the three allies had to make were considerable, and in the case of France, they greatly complicated the fiscal burdens of the monarchy.[5]

Although France and Spain initially sought to help the American colonists by launching a massive attack on the British naval base at Portsmouth in the summer of 1779, the failure of that plan and the Marquis of Lafayette's lobbying for effective military aid on the American continent led the French to equip and send an expeditionary force.[6] Lieutenant-General Jean-Baptiste Donatien Rochambeau was appointed commander of the six thousand men sent to serve as an auxiliary force to the American armies. He was instructed to lead the corps as a separate unit but to follow American directives. In case the Americans were defeated and their armies destroyed, the contingency plan was to evacuate the French soldiers to Hispaniola.[7]

The expedition was slated to sail from Brest in the early spring of 1780, but the exasperating delays and petty infighting ensured that the fleet did not set out into the open Atlantic until the beginning of May.[8] They reached Newport in Rhode Island on July 11. Although at first there were misunderstandings on how best to use the French expeditionary corps, it was the decisive participation of the French fleet and army in the siege of Yorktown that eventually turned the balance of the war in favor of American independence.[9]

First Caribbean Repercussions

In Curaçao, according to Cornelius Goslinga, the American Revolutionary War had the effect of promoting the development of the island:

> [T]he island became not only a commercial center for the entire Caribbean, but a cosmopolitan meeting place where pirates, American rebels, not too respectable Dutchmen, upright Spaniards, and creole grandees from the coast rubbed shoulders.[10]

The characterization that Goslinga makes of the island's frequenters may tend to the exotic, but it highlights a reality. Revolutions set many people into motion, not only at their epicenters but also at the margins. The 8,500 inhabitants of Curaçao managed in 1795 to resist for a time the French Republic's pressure to annex the island, but the following year the Batavian Republic to which Curaçao belonged was united to France, and Curaçao became entangled in the vicissitudes of the Anglo-French wars for the next two decades. It was difficult to step away from the revolutionary turmoil of the times.[11]

In the French- and Spanish-speaking Caribbean, the dissemination of North American revolutionary ideas was not as evident. The fact that France and Spain, as well as the Netherlands, became allies of the American revolutionaries opened the Caribbean ports to the Americans and, as Goslinga pointed out, livened up the encounters of traders and sailors with the host societies in Curaçao.[12]

Why Was Saint-Domingue the Strongest Focus of Revolution?

Concerned with the inhabitants' smuggling relations with the Dutch, the Spanish authorities in the early seventeenth century had ordered the removal of all the population from the western and northwestern coasts of the island of Hispaniola, their first colony in the New

World. Even promising settlements, like Puerto Plata, were depopulated.[13] For many Dominican historians, this forcible removal of the population in the seventeenth century had dire consequences for the evolution of Dominican society.

Feral cattle and pigs, left behind by the evicted settlers, multiplied. Pirates and corsairs, who frequented the coast because it was a convenient point to stop between forays on Spanish ships returning to Seville, began to provision themselves with the abundant source of meat. Some migratory population, especially French, began to settle the area to hunt down the animals and trade their meat with the pirates. From the exercise of their profession (*boucaner,* to cure meat) they became known as *boucaniers,* or buccaneers. Eventually bands of pirates settled the nearby island of Tortuga. They were known as freebooters, because they made compacts of brotherhood to share risks and booty. Historians distinguish freebooters from pirates on the basis of the contractual bonds that linked the first, and pirates from corsairs (privateers in American tradition), as the latter were granted a patent or charter from an established government allowing them and their crews to prey on enemy ships and settlements during a war. In practice, as some historians have shown, the same person could be a pirate, a freebooter, or a privateer in different stages of his life. Some of them became prominent public figures, like Henry Morgan, who was named governor of Jamaica, or Charles d'Angennes, Marquis of Maintenon, who was governor of Marie Galante.[14]

Eventually the French crown became interested in the thriving settlement on Hispaniola, and it sponsored a commercial society that began settling and cultivating the southwestern part. By dint of promises and maneuvers the crown, which eventually superseded the company's interests, obtained the grudging assent of most buccaneers and freebooters to abide by the established laws in exchange for amnesty and recognition of their claims and interests. A treaty with Spain delimited an area under French jurisdiction, which began to be called Saint-Domingue. Thus the island was formally partitioned in two jurisdictions, the French and the Spanish.

While the Spanish part of the island languished, on account of the lack of investment capital and trade (it was much more lucrative for

Spanish venture capitalists to invest in Mexico, Peru, or Venezuela), the French rapidly developed their part of the island as the jewel of their colonial empire. The commercial houses in Bordeaux, Nantes, Saint-Malo, and other French Atlantic ports invested in the development of the fertile valleys of the island, which were planted in sugarcane and indigo, while the hills were planted with coffee groves.[15] In spite of the French exclusivist trade regulations for the colonies, the French crown liberalized laws in the 1760s and allowed certain ports to deal with foreigners, notably Mole-Saint-Nicholas in Saint-Domingue.[16]

The labor came from Africa, in vast quantities, so that on the eve of the revolution there were almost half a million slaves in the colony. The tropical products went to France, from which some of them were processed or refined (in the case of black sugar or molasses) and distributed throughout northern Europe. A minority of planters became very rich. Others were indebted to French commercial houses. But there were also a sizable number of Frenchmen who had not become members of the planting and trading elite. They were government functionaries, professionals, small merchants, or farmers. Beyond them there were French artisans and workers, and further beyond there were drifters and displaced landowners, war veterans, and incapacitated people, who occasionally made their discontent manifest. Several strong clashes between the different segments of the French population occurred much before the revolution started in France.[17] In the British-ruled islands, the poorer European population had tended to move on to North America or to other places once all the land had been appropriated and large estates constituted. In Saint-Domingue there were not many emigration outlets for the European poor.

Saint-Domingue, in contrast to the British-ruled islands, had a large population of free people of color, some 30,000 by 1789. The racial barrier was not as high among the French as among the English, although it was higher than in the Spanish colonies.[18] Many Frenchmen recognized the children they had from their unions with African or island-born Creole women. Often they emancipated their children and left bequests for them. Other African workers gained their freedom through their work, either by savings or through compensations accorded to them. In the Roman law tradition, slaves were allowed to buy their freedom, and those legal institutions permitted a number of free colored workers in both the French and Spanish islands to obtain their freedom. No such legal tradition prevailed in the British Caribbean. As a consequence of these practices, not only were there many free men and women of color in Saint-Domingue, but some of them were landowners—and among them, they had more than 100,000 slaves of their own.[19]

But in 1788–89, these free people were excluded from the deliberative assemblies that prepared the Cahier de Doléances for the colony of Saint-Domingue. The Cahier was a compendium of petitions to be sent to the Estates-General, which King Louis XVI had convoked in Versailles for May 1789. After the Estates-General defied the king and constituted themselves as a national assembly, and the people of Paris forestalled the attempt to deploy troops to intimidate the assembly by storming the Bastille, the echoes of these events shook the colony. As successive news from France reached Saint-Domingue, the poorer Frenchmen began to agitate for greater participation in the National Guard and in the municipal councils that were formed. Fearing for the loss of their privileges, a group of planters obtained from the Ministry of Marine (which oversaw the colonies) to have a colonial assembly elected. The property qualifications to vote were such that the planters gained control of it.[20]

When news broke that the French National Assembly, in August 1789, had approved the Declaration of the Rights of Man, the free people of color heightened their demands to participate in public affairs. They drew up their own Cahier, whose first article declared:

> The inhabitants of the French colonies are uniquely and generally distributed and divided in two classes, that of free men, and that of men who are born and live in slavery.[21]

They proceeded to elect their own delegates to the National Assembly in France, much to the chagrin of the European French on the island, who began lobbying that these delegates would not be recognized in Paris. Thus the main political struggle in Saint-Domingue was no longer between rich and poor Frenchmen, but between whites and free people of color.

In the fall of 1790, Vincent Ogé, who had been to France to lobby for the recognition of the equal rights of the free people of color and had returned to Saint-Domingue with little hope that the government would act, led a rebellion against the local authorities. Defeated and handed over by the Spanish when he fled to the other part of the island, he was publicly executed on February 25, 1791, with a fellow leader, Jean-Baptiste Chavannes. The cruelty of the execution, however, provoked animosities both locally and in France.[22]

In May 1791, a Jacobin deputy named Rabell obtained from the French Assembly the passage of a decree that enfranchised mulattoes who had property qualifications and were born of free parents.[23] Although in practice it only allowed a tiny minority of free people of color to vote, the decree provoked fury in Saint-Domingue.

But while the colonists debated the participation of the free people of color in the revolutionary institutions, the almost half a million slaves, many of them of African birth, began to move. On the night of August 22, 1791, the slave rebellion began, in the name of the King of France. It soon spread to most parts of the colony. One of the prominent leaders in the early phase was Jean-François. Attaching himself to this leader in September as "Physician in Chief to the Armies of the King of France" was a forty-eight-year-old slave plantation overseer, Toussaint L'Ouverture.[24]

Negotiations to end the rebellion did not succeed, in part because the local authorities could not fathom the strength of the movement and believed it could easily be put down. Meanwhile in France, the revolution was becoming more radical, and members of the French aristocracy began to leave and seek refuge in England, Germany, or elsewhere. From their places of refuge they sponsored resistance to the revolution and advocated for the intervention of other European powers to restore the king of France's absolute government.

The Colonial Assembly meeting in Cap Français rejected the equality of political rights for mulattoes. The slave rebellion became more radical. As Fick comments:

The French Revolution did provide the political conditions within which autonomous slave rebellion could fairly rapidly assume revolutionary proportions, and without the French Revolution there would have been no talk of liberty and equality, no counterrevolution, no ready access to allies and arms for the slaves.[25]

In 1792, the French Legislative Assembly sent to Saint-Domingue three peace commissioners with an army of two thousand regular troops and six thousand National Guards.[26] Some rebel leaders were intimidated by the news of the coming of such a contingent and sought means of extricating themselves from the rebellion.

Royalist planters from Saint-Domingue, as well as from other islands, sought help in Great Britain in December 1792. The occasion was opportune because Great Britain was weighing a declaration of war in response to the French revolutionary army's invasion of Austrian Flanders. The idea of depriving France of its Caribbean islands appealed to British ruling circles, so that as soon as the war against France started, the British dispatched an expeditionary force to Saint-Domingue. They also occupied the other French islands in the Eastern Caribbean. In Saint-Domingue, however, the British experience was harsh.

Spain also declared war on France, and recruited the slave rebels as allies against the French expeditionary force in Saint-Domingue.[27] Thus the French found themselves on the defensive. The situation became desperate as the combined slave and Spanish forces cut off the French in the North from the rest of the island, while the British occupied some of the ports and plains of the center and south. It was at this juncture that the French Convention, which had succeeded the Legislative Assembly and abolished the monarchy, sent Léger-Félicité Sonthonax and two other commissioners, Etienne Polverel and Jean-Antoine Bilhaud, to seek a solution in Haiti. Bilhaud soon fell ill and Polverel took Sonthonax's lead, so that the thirty-year-old deputy gathered in his hands all the initiative. Sonthonax sized up the desperate situation and made a desperate gamble. On August 29, 1793, he unilaterally declared the emancipation of all slaves in Saint-Domingue.[28] He negotiated with the rebel leaders their return to

French allegiance. Of the leaders who accepted his proposition, Toussaint L'Ouverture was the most important. He handed over to the French the territories his forces occupied and turned his forces against the Spanish.

The French Convention, although surprised at Sonthonax's move, agreed on February 4, 1794, to abolish slavery.[29] It was a means of turning the tables against the British, who had occupied the eastern Caribbean islands. Not only was British rule in those islands subverted by the Convention's decree, but the word of abolition also spread among the slaves in the British-ruled islands and caused some unrest. French planters were left with Great Britain as their only hope of recovering their property, and many of them became counter-revolutionaries, exposing themselves to reprisals when Guadeloupe was retaken by the French under General Victor Hughes.

Although Sonthonax was recalled to France in June 1794, he was able to convince his fellow delegates in the Convention of the rightness of his decisions in Saint-Domingue. Sonthonax was again sent to Saint-Domingue, this time by a commission of the minister of colonies.[30]

Sonthonax tried to maintain the balance of power in Saint-Domingue. When the Peace of Basel took Spain out of the war in the summer of 1795, pressure from that side disappeared. The Spanish, who had agreed to cede their part of the island to the French under article 9 of the treaty,[31] sought a refuge for their Saint-Dominguan ex-slave allies in Florida, where they stayed until that colony was sold to the United States in 1819.[32]

Although Sonthonax faced internal opposition from several factions, he maintained the administration of Saint-Domingue on an even keel by persuading former slaves to work for wages or provisions in some plantations, fomenting exports through Cap Français and giving patents to privateers, who used Santiago de Cuba and Campeche as ports where they could liquidate their prizes. Toussaint gained the confidence of Sonthonax, who began delegating military powers on him. Eventually, when Sonthonax was recalled to France the second time, he left Toussaint as commander in chief of a combination of troops, most of which were composed of former slaves.

Toussaint made two bold moves: he occupied Spanish Santo Domingo, and he convoked a constitutional convention, which in 1801 drew up a constitution for the French colony of Saint-Domingue. Its twenty-eighth article read:

> The constitution names as governor citizen Toussaint L'Ouverture, general in chief of the army of Saint-Domingue, and in consideration to the important services which the general has rendered to the colony, in the most critical circumstances of the revolution, and through the desire of the grateful inhabitants, its reins are entrusted to him for the rest of his glorious life.[33]

In France, intense lobbying by dispossessed planters and by other elements moved First Consul Napoleon Bonaparte to plan a sizable expedition to assert French authority in the colony, and although it was not explicitly stated at the moment, to re-establish slavery. The command of this expedition was entrusted to Napoleon's brother-in-law, General Charles Victor-Emmanuel Leclerc. The Peace of Amiens in 1801 between France and Great Britain had removed the threat of the British fleet, so that 10,500 soldiers were able to embark at Brest and other ports, and they arrived in Saint-Domingue in February 1802.[34] Leclerc was able to obtain Toussaint's surrender; he was sent to prison in France where he died.

Leclerc initially thought his work of suppressing the rebellion would be quickly accomplished,[35] and he even obtained the cooperation of some of Toussaint's subordinates, like Jean-Jacques Dessalines. Eventually, however, the suspicion spread among the former insurgents that Leclerc's true agenda was the re-establishment of slavery, which at the time was being pursued in Martinique and Guadeloupe. The black troops rebelled, Dessalines assumed their command, and the war again became fierce. Yellow fever, which at an earlier period had decimated invading British troops, spread rapidly among the French troops. Leclerc himself died of it in November 1802. His successor, Rochambeau, was unable to save the situation. War with Great Britain broke out again in May 1803. The British came to besiege Rochambeau, who surrendered to them in November 1803. The stage was set for the declaration of independence of Haiti, which Dessalines decreed in 1804.

The Haitian Revolution in a Wider Context

What is common to the revolutions arising on the Atlantic shores of Europe and America between 1765 and 1830 analyzed by Godechot and Palmer are their demographic, economic, and ideological elements. The traditional institutions shattered under the pressures caused by the unprecedented growth in population in the eighteenth century. The commercial and cultural links of the time spread the results of the local conflicts throughout the Atlantic world. It was predictable that people compared other societies' struggles with their own.

The American Revolution was not an isolated phenomenon. As Palmer has shown, there is a common revolutionary ambiance that links revolutions as disparate as that of the city of Geneva in the 1760s and the revolutionary movements spurred by French troops marching throughout Europe three and four decades later. What historians of the Atlantic Revolution have been reluctant to consider has been the nexus between the revolutionary movements in the North Atlantic and those that arose in Haiti and in Spanish America out of their contact with the previous revolutions. When one reads Francisco de Miranda's diary of his trip in the 1780s through the recently independent states of North America,[x] or the reminiscences of Simón Bolívar of his travels in Europe twenty years later, one becomes aware that the contacts between the revolutionary movements in South America and the North Atlantic are not casual.

The French Revolution, therefore, should be seen as part of a continuum, and in a larger context than that of Bourbon France. In the Caribbean, its influence is first felt on the French islands, especially the colony of Saint-Domingue. There the Declaration of Human Rights of the French National Assembly in August 1789 polarized society in two different ways. For the French planters, who initially dominated local assemblies, the distinction of color was paramount, and by refusing to admit free men of color to their deliberations, they detonated the first revolutionary conflict. For the free people of color, the dividing line was the condition of personal freedom. Whether to set apart people on the basis of civil condition or of race eventually became moot as slaves took up their own cause. Rising first in the name of King Louis XVI, and afterward on their own right, they began that slow, painful, contradictory, and destructive process that eventually led to the declaration of Haitian independence in 1804.

Then the very state of war between France and Great Britain, from 1793 on, involved the English-speaking islands in the discussion of the revolutionary tenets. According to David Geggus,

> the basic facts of the Haitian Revolution seem to have been rapidly disseminated along regional trade routes. Sailors, refugees, and proselytizing privateers spread tales of apocalyptic destruction and a new world in the making and planters everywhere voiced fears of another Saint Domingue. From Jamaica to Trinidad, slaves celebrated in song the triumph of the Haitian insurgents. In 1800, the year Toussaint Louverture became governor of Saint Domingue, slaves sang in the streets of Kingston, "Black, white, brown. . . . All the same."[37]

The very fact that the British, in the face of the new strain of yellow fever they encountered in Saint-Domingue that decimated their troops (as well as the French), had to resort to buying African slaves outright for the purpose of forming regiments suddenly gave rise to a whole new range of discussions.[38]

Finally, the Spanish islands woke up to the debates in spite of the Crown's efforts to shield them from ideological influences, as Spain became embroiled first in a war against France and later, as an ally of France, against Great Britain. An early manifestation of the revolutionary fervor was the Conspiracy of Coro of 1795, in which the commercial links between Saint-Domingue and Venezuela showed that trade could be the means by which revolutionary ideas were disseminated.[39] On the outskirts of Coro, the rumor spread among the slaves that King Charles IV had made them free, but that the slave owners were not complying with the royal order. The rumor had its origin in a visit to Spain made by José Caridad González, an African freedman who was litigating the possession of untitled lands and obtained a favorable royal decree. He led a militia company of free blacks in an uprising in Coro, which resulted in some three dozen deaths, including his own, and the eventual execution of its leader, José Leonardo Chirino. The son of a slave and an Indian woman, Chirino was a free man, day laborer, and sharecropper who had traveled to Saint-Domingue with his father-in-law. In the uprising, Chirino had proclaimed "the law of the French."[40]

Another illustration of this slow-motion development of the French revolutionary influence was a movement that arose among Dominica's slaves in 1791. The island had belonged to France, and Great Britain did not desire to return it at the Treaty of Versailles in 1783, which put an official end to the War of the American Revolution. A mulatto from Martinique, Jean-Louis Polinaire, stirred the slaves with revolutionary propaganda:

> The uprising was unique in the history of the West Indian slave revolts. What the slaves under Polinaire's influence were demanding was freedom to work for themselves for more days in the week, as well as the customary one and a half days on weekends. When this demand was refused the slaves virtually went on strike without going off the estates or attempting any acts of violence.[41]

Polinaire was captured on March 7, 1791, and the authorities hanged him, quartered his body, and hung the parts as a warning to slaves.

The Haitian Revolution has been the one that historians have been most reluctant to accept within the Atlantic revolutionary paradigm.[42] The fact that it was a slave revolution isolated it at the time from the other libertarian movements, but what has been curious is that it is still isolated two centuries after the events by the historiography of the period. The exceptionality that has been imposed on the history of the Haitian Revolution has reflected the malevolence of the slaveholding regions before the consummated fact in Haiti.

In the beginning of the nineteenth century, the fear of Haiti was widespread. One only has to read the record of debates in the United

States Congress, in its deliberation over the sending of emissaries to the Congress of Panama in 1826, to become aware that the quarantine then imposed on Haiti still has its effect on the historiography of the American continent.[43]

It is interesting to note that in both the English- and Spanish-speaking islands, measures were taken to avoid the spread of news of the Haitian Revolution among the slaves. In Cuba, according to Johanna Von Grafenstein, who cites the work of Michael Zeuske and Clarence Munford, the fear of Haiti's influence was manipulated

> by the Cuban oligarchs to obtain greater control over the free blacks and mulattoes. At the same time, concrete measures were taken to confront the danger of possible slave rebellions. According to the authors cited [Zeuske and Munford], the real danger of a "contagion" was minimal in comparison with the positive strengthening effect that the fall of coffee and sugar production in the neighboring French colony had on the Cuban economy.[44]

In a circular letter dated at the end of 1805, Toribio de Montes, the governor of Puerto Rico, advised local authorities on the subject of "a suspicious French mulatto named Chantallatte," eighteen to twenty years of age, who was thought to be an emissary from Dessalines ("that black notoriously [who] revolted in the Island of Santo Domingo"). Chantallatte must be sought and held "before he spills his damned seed on an island which enjoys the most perfect tranquility, loyalty and honor."[45]

In January 1806, Montes again warned local authorities to watch several black and mulatto envoys from Santo Domingo, sent "by the General of their color." At the end of January 1806, he again charged the local authorities with vigilance:

> Clandestine insurgent blacks of the Island of Santo Domingo have committed themselves to propagate the disorder in which they live by means of emissaries and secret correspondence, not only to introduce the same evils in the neighboring islands, but also to spread themselves among them.[46]

Montes gave as evidence the confession obtained under torture from a slave in Trinidad, and he added:

> From other islands secret warnings have been sent with denunciations of people of color who are here working against subordination, against slavery and against order. These evils become enormous, as we have seen in the French possessions in this America. . . . Either by fortune or by vigilance which has prevailed at all times, no machination . . . has been discovered here, but it is time to take some measures. . . . The greatest vigilance must be undertaken against suspicion, malice and weakness. Not only must it be exercised over slaves, but also over the foreign free of color, alien to this most loyal island, and over all, on the wanderers, shiftless, ex-convicts and deserters, who are capable of seducing, advising and being the first . . . to commence brigandage.[47]

In November 1807, Montes evoked a royal decree:

> It has come to the King's notice that some emissaries from Dessalines have departed from Santo Domingo to organize a slave revolution in the American settlements of the European powers. His Majesty wants that every man of color, when he arrives from Santo Domingo to the Spanish colonies, be immediately arrested, as well as the residents with whom those emissaries may have communication.[48]

The fear of Haitian influence also had its uses. When New Spain's revolutionaries sought to dissuade Spanish authorities in Cuba from sponsoring royalist movements, they warned them that the cost of their support to such movements would be a Cuban slave uprising fostered by Haitian authorities. Vicente Rocafuerte, Mexico's envoy to London, wrote:

> Santo Domingo is the terror of the Island of Cuba. Let us profit from the alliance which can be made with [Haitian leader Jean-Pierre] Boyer to assume a menacing attitude and make Spaniards in Havana understand, that if they invade us, they too will be invaded; that if they come to Mexico to put an end to anarchy, as they say, we too will go to Cuba to put an end to the slavery of blacks.[49]

General Ferrand and the French Occupation of Spanish Santo Domingo

Battle at Santo Domingo.

One of the many thousands of Frenchmen who volunteered to serve the king of France in his American war was twenty-one-year-old Marie-Louis Ferrand, a younger brother of one of the French surgeons in the expedition. Born in Besançon on December 13, 1758, he was the son of Louis Ferrand, an officer at the local bureau of the mint, and Anne-Marie-Françoise Varin.[1] According to one account, he accompanied his older brother the surgeon; and according to another, he started out as a sublieutenant on the French privateer *La Duchesse de Chartres* and then served on the French expeditionary force as a quartermaster's inspector from 1781 to 1783.

Upon his return to France, the younger Ferrand joined the Dauphin's Regiment at Angers and served until February 1788, when he obtained his release from the force. Between 1789 and 1792, he served as a grenadier of the National Guard in Paris. By September 1792, he was a cavalry lieutenant in the Twenty-fourth Cavalry Regiment and the following year he transferred to the Twenty-fifth Regiment as squadron chief.[2] In 1793, at the height of the Reign of Terror, he was arrested under suspicion of favoring the suppressed monarchy.[3] After the Terror, he returned to military service; and in 1794, he became brigade general and was active in the west of France. He married Marie-Anne-Eulalie Chevalier. Ferrand became commander of the garrison at Valenciennes after the Peace of Amiens, then of Calais, and he volunteered to go to Santo Domingo when General Leclerc's army was sent to take control of the island from Toussaint L'Ouverture. He received command of the troops operating on the former Spanish side of the island, in the department of Cibao, and as such he fought against Dessalines's troops in 1803.[4]

For the French, after they succeeded in obtaining Toussaint L'Ouverture's capture and removal to France, the Saint-Domingue campaign went downhill. The uprising of the troops that had been loyal to L'Ouverture, Dessalines's fateful change of sides to favor the insurgents, the spread of yellow fever among the French troops, and finally General Leclerc's death of that plague had been a series of unmitigated disasters.[5] General Donatien Marie-Joseph Rochambeau, son of the leader of the American expedition in 1780, took over command after Leclerc's death, but the draconian measures he took against the insurgents just added more rage to the conflict. When Rochambeau had to seek terms to evacuate his troops from the island by surrendering to the British at the end of 1803, General Ferrand was left isolated in the Spanish part. Pressed by Dessalines, he started retreating from the valley of the Cibao.

Ferrand Takes Command of Santo Domingo

The object of General Ferrand's painful retreat from the military post of Montechristi was the fortified city of Santo Domingo. Here Ferrand made a move that some have qualified as a coup d'état. He displaced the commanding general Kerversau and assumed the rule of the old

Spanish part of the island. As he communicated it to his immediate subordinate, General Barquier, Ferrand, although of equal rank to Kerversau, was his senior by six months in military service, and by seniority he was entitled to the command.[6] Behind his action lay latent the presumption that Kerversau would not act decisively in the urgent circumstances.

That Ferrand had the desire to command his subsequent actions fully demonstrated. He took charge of all the pertinent decisions to lodge his troops, feed them, and keep them ready for action. He sent dispatches to the authorities in the neighboring Spanish islands and the metropolitan French authorities. And he started preparations for the eventual defense of the city against the expected attack of the rebels of Saint-Domingue.

The Militia Commanders

The keystone for Ferrand's plans was the reorganization of Santo Domingo's Creole militia. He sought the most apt commanders for the different districts, and especially he recruited former officers of the Spanish army who had remained on the island. Of them, Manuel Peralta, a native of Granada, had joined the Spanish army in 1770, had served in South America between 1776 and 1778, and had served in the Gibraltar campaign during the American Revolutionary War between 1779 and 1781. He had returned to Hispaniola in 1782 and served in the Spanish part of the island.[7] In 1789 Peralta, who was adjutant major of the six companies of dragoon militia, attained the title of captain. After the cession of Santo Domingo to France, he requested in 1798 from the Spanish royal government that he be allowed to stay on the island, since his aged father-in-law, Antonio Mañón, was having difficulties in disposing of his many possessions in the eventuality of emigrating from the island. The Crown gave him license for a year, but with renewable extensions, and formally inscribed him in the cavalry militia of Caracas.[8] Still in Santo Domingo in April 1802, Peralta obtained from the Spanish Crown the favor that his sons could join any of the military corps in America, with dispensation for being underage, but without right to seniority.[9] Ferrand charged Peralta with the command of the militia in the department of Ozama and granted him the rank of chief of brigade.[10] With Peralta, Ferrand developed a relationship of full confidence, which ran through the five years of his exercise as governor.

Another Spanish officer in Ferrand's circle was José Ruiz, born in Cartagena in Spain in 1774. General Kerversau had named him ship's lieutenant in 1803, and Ferrand gave him command of the militia in the districts west of the capital. Besides watching out for the incursions of the Saint-Domingue rebels, Ruiz had the mission of maintaining harmony and encouragement among the principal landholders of the zone and, as far as possible, of attracting them to service in the militia. At the beginning of 1808, Ruiz broke with Ferrand, apparently because he did not get an expected promotion in rank, and departed for Puerto Rico.

From early on in Ferrand's official correspondence, one can observe that it had become particularly hard to attract Ciriaco Ramírez, from Cádiz, to serve in the militia. One cannot trust him, Ferrand stated in a communication early in 1804, but it is necessary to steer him.[11] To Ramírez, Ferrand had trusted the defense of Azúa against the forces of Dessalines, insisting to him that against this common enemy a perfect unity of efforts be maintained.[12] When Ramírez later avoided communicating with Ferrand, the latter reminded him of the benefits that residents of Santo Domingo derived from French rule and added the rhetorical question "Doesn't the shame of living under the orders of men who were your slaves amount to anything?"[13] When Ramírez finally answered, Ferrand tried to consolidate his support:

> I rely on you, citizen commander, to help me and [C]ommander Ruiz, in our well-defined intentions to contribute to the happiness of the inhabitants of the former Spanish part, while we busy ourselves in the interests of the government we serve.[14]

In May 1805, Ferrand tried to iron out the differences with the inhabitants of Azúa, who were somewhat reluctant to follow his instructions. It seemed that Ciriaco Ramírez was at the bottom of the resistance. "I am persuaded of his good intentions," Ferrand wrote in a letter to a Señor González in Azúa,

> and I count you among those to whom I grant my trust to re-establish order in the district of Azúa. I have reason to believe that Ciriaco Ramírez has not measured up to the trust of his fellow citizens, and on account of that, I am disillusioned.[15]

Ferrand had an easier relationship with the commandant of Bani. As for Santiago and the rest of the Cibao district, the repeated incursions from the rebels' territory spurred frequent communications with Santo Domingo.

The relations with the other militia commanders of the island were shaped by the needs of the moment. With the commander of Monte Grande, Silvestre Aybar, the relations were stable. Thus on June 10, 1808, Ferrand wrote to him about a road that was being planned that would be of utility to the inhabitants of his district, and as late as October 23 of that year, he wrote to Aybar to promote the provisioning of corn and rice, since wheat flour was becoming dear.[16]

With Diego de Lira, the commander of Savana la Mar, the correspondence was just as cordial. In the spring of 1804, Ferrand wrote to him urging him to watch for illegal emigration from Savana la Mar, so that those who had passports left the island only through Santo Domingo. He commended to him the administration of local justice until a council of notables be established at Savana la Mar.[17] In the summer of 1804, Ferrand wrote to him again, this time to follow up on a matter concerning a church rent.[18]

The War against the Haitians

By a decree in the summer of 1804, Ferrand established the area effectively ruled by the French, from Puerto Caballo on the northern coast to Cap Beata on the southern coast.[19] All ships trading to the west of those limits would be considered fair prize for privateers.

Throughout the time of his command, Ferrand did not lose opportunities to inflict damage on the rebels, whom he ever called *brigands*, or bandits. Hardly had the siege of Santo Domingo lifted in 1805 when Ferrand wrote to General Theureau, then in Philadelphia, that a man named Bunel, Dessalines's agent in the United States and living in Philadelphia

> is the man who [inflicts the most damage] on this colony of Saint-Domingue and it would be an inestimable advantage if he were captured. With two thousand *gourdes*, M. General, you would easily achieve it. This is what I am writing to the Minister, advising him that I will take care of it, if you are not successful.[20]

When a Haitian privateer ship was captured near Puerto Plata, Ferrand ordered that its captain be brought to Santo Domingo to be interrogated ("I don't think it is necessary to bring him to a court-martial") and then had him hanged.[21] Meanwhile the rest of the ship's crew was massacred in Puerto Plata.

At the beginning of 1808, Ferrand wrote to Colonel Franco, the commandant of the department of Cibao, that the differences prevalent "in the country occupied by the rebels offer the opportunity to make some move against the Mirabelais, and I think that Etienne Albert, seconded by Francisco Esteves and Marcos Torres, could render us in these circumstances essential services."[22] But the letter did not reach Franco in time, because he had left Santiago, and Ferrand then wrote to Etienne Albert and sent another letter to Franco.[23] Apparently, Ferrand sought to create a diversion while he himself essayed an incursion into Saint-Domingue at the end of March. What happened, however, was that Ferrand ended making an inspection of the department of the Cibao.[24]

Licenses to Privateers

The imperative need to find resources to maintain the army led Ferrand to explore all available alternatives. In previous wars, France had licensed privateers (*corsaires*) who captured commercial shipping belonging to enemy states.[25] There was an established procedure to determine if the captured ship was a legitimate seizure. If the determination was affirmative, the ship and its merchandise were auctioned. To finance his campaign for the retaking of the islands of Guadeloupe and Martinique, General Victor Hugues had licensed privateers who captured 358 ships between 1795 and 1801. With the revenues from these prizes, Hugues was able not only to pay the expenses of his army but also to enrich all the participants in the project.[26] Similarly, when Sonthonax sought means to support the regime of the Convention in Saint-Domingue in the 1790s, he commissioned privateers who sold their prizes in Santiago, Havana, and Campeche.[27]

Part of the difficulty Ferrand had was that Hugues's successors in Guadeloupe continued the lucrative licensing. Many times, the privateers sought ships in the waters of old Saint-Domingue, where those who traded with the rebels constituted legitimate prizes. Ferrand tried without much success to restrict the competition from Guadeloupe to the eastern Caribbean.[28]

Other sources of difficulties were constituted procedures to determine fair prizes. The captains of the seized ships used all manner of arguments to forestall the appropriation of their boats. Many of them were North Americans who frequented the ports of Jacmel and Cap Haitien (renamed from Cap Français). In 1805, Ferrand wrote to the minister of marine and colonies that the moment the commercial relations between the Americans and the rebels ceased, it would be easy to end the war of Saint-Domingue, "and I am truly convinced that all that is needed is a word from His Imperial Majesty." If Ferrand had a few ships at his disposal, he would sweep from the sea the American interlopers in Saint-Domingue.[29]

But Ferrand also wanted to keep up good relations with North American traders. He hoped to attract them to Santo Domingo to foster the development of the Spanish part of the island. In September 1804, Ferrand intervened to release a brig captained by a North American friend named Taggard, whom he sought to link to Santo Domingo's legitimate trade.[30]

The principal hindrance to making the licensing of privateers a lucrative enterprise was the final disposition of the prizes. Obviously

in Santo Domingo itself, the necessary capital for the profitable auc-
tion of the ships and their cargoes was no longer available. On the
other hand, a British squadron constantly patrolled the waters of
Santo Domingo and could seize the privateers and their captured
ships if they tried to make it around the island to bring their prizes
there from the neighborhood of the cape. Ferrand recurred to the old
ententes for these matters between Spain and France. The privateers
he licensed would take their prizes to the ports of Cuba and Puerto
Rico to dispose of the ships and their cargoes there.

The problem that Ferrand confronted was the desire of the Spanish
authorities in those islands to reap much higher percentages of the
profits than those contemplated. In particular, he denounced the
exactions of the port authorities in Mayaguez. These difficulties led
Ferrand to make the decision to have the privateers dispose of their
prizes in other jurisdictions, notably Saint Thomas, but the presence
of the British squadron made the easy access to Puerto Rico hard to
resist.

Of all the prizes that were acquired under Ferrand's government of
Santo Domingo, the most profitable was an accidental one—the capture of a damaged Danish slave ship stranded on the eastern coast of
the island, near Higuey. Ferrand rapidly put forth the idea that the
cargo constituted a fair prize and set up a commission to adjudicate
the claim.[31] The sale of the approximately six hundred slaves it carried produced the greatest gain that the Ferrand administration
enjoyed from its sponsorship of privateers.

The Sale of Church Goods

The sale of liturgical vessels, reliquaries, and other precious objects
belonging to the churches in Spanish Santo Domingo constituted
another source of funds. When he learned of the cession of the
Spanish territory to France under the Treaty of Basel of 1795,
Archbishop Portillo of Santo Domingo ordered that all sacred objects
be gathered from the churches to remove them from the island
before the French took possession.[32] Nevertheless, Toussaint

L'Ouverture occupied Santo Domingo in the name of France before the warehoused items could be sent to Spain or to some other part of the Spanish dominions. When Ferrand took possession of the city, the assemblage of all the sacred vessels in the capital turned out to be highly convenient. He sent a portion of them to the French agent in Saint Thomas, to attempt selling there the objects, or if not, to melt them for their silver and gold content.[33] Another portion remained stockpiled in Santo Domingo, and Ferrand gradually yielded pieces from this lot to the few priests who had remained in the colony so that they could use them for worship.

Neither the income derived from privateers nor that from the sale of ecclesiastical goods was sufficient to cover the recurring expenses of the French army. The administration in Santo Domingo, in its perpetual search for funds, pretended to obtain credit in Saint Thomas, Curaçao, Caracas, and Philadelphia, ever invoking the support of the French treasury. Ferrand's correspondence shows how frequently he pressed the metropolitan authorities so that Santo Domingo's credit stayed liquid in America.[34]

On the other hand, Ferrand's communications with his agent in Saint Thomas reveal the French contingent's needs. Ferrand, claiming that his troops went practically barefoot, repeatedly implored for the remittance of five hundred pairs of shoes. Neither was there ever enough flour available. Thus in 1805, Ferrand wrote to the governor of the Danish Virgin Islands requesting as a special favor the dispatch of flour, because the expected shipment had not arrived from the United States.[35] Cloth to make shirts and sufficient rum for the troops were other requests Ferrand made to Saint Thomas. Officers, however, supplied themselves with wine. The supply of beef for the troops was a recurrent problem, and the plains near the capital were not always able provide it.

The Haitian Siege of Santo Domingo

Recurrent rumors of an expedition by Dessalines to Santo Domingo had reached Ferrand's ears throughout 1804. On several occasions, he urged the local commandants to make forays into the rebels' territory. At the beginning of 1805, a circular letter that has become legendary urged the execution of rebel prisoners older than sixteen years and the sale of minors as slaves, preferably to the United States.

In March 1805, Ferrand wrote to his subordinate Pichot that Henri Christophe, one of Dessalines's subordinate officers, was camping in front of Santiago. He reminded him that Dessalines was attempting to enter by Azúa, and he added:

> Although I am convinced that they will not reach Santo Domingo, we should nevertheless neglect nothing, so that we are not caught unprepared, and I am requesting of you the greatest dispatch for all the measures that the defense of the city demands, whose command is entrusted to you.[36]

Three days later, Ferrand instructed Peralta to give orders to the commanders of Monteplata, Bayaguana, and Seybo to have all their available militias ready to put themselves under the orders of Juan Baron, who was in charge of the reconnaissance of the Santiago route.[37] Ferrand received a report from Baron two days later saying that the rebels were in Cotui. Ferrand told his aide Vives to order the unloading of provisions, cloth, and goods necessary for the siege from all the ships anchored in the port but reserving in them all that was necessary to feed the people who had to leave Santo Domingo. "This measure requires so much more speed, since I would like to have all the unnecessary civilians (*toutes les bouches inutiles*) depart tomorrow, if it is possible."[38]

Two days later, Ferrand complained to Pichot that instead of diminishing, the number of slaves in the city had risen. He ordered their departure, as well as that of the free people of color who had come in from the countryside, who should be embarked to the eastern part of the island.[39] When the siege started two days later, Ferrand ordered the chief engineer to destroy the houses by the port, to give the artillery some room.[40]

Ferrand wrote to the French consul in Charlestown, asking him to send French soldiers who may be found there from those who had belonged to the late general Leclerc's expeditionary corps. He explained,

Dessalines is at the gates of Santo Domingo with ten thousand men. I have reason to believe that I will keep the city for time enough to make this enterprise detestable to him, and that this event will wind up being advantageous to the Government, but we need provisions and some men.[41]

Dessalines placed some barricades on San Carlos, and Ferrand prompted General Barquier to make a reconnaissance of them with a force of three hundred infantrymen and thirty cavalry.[42] Two days later Ferrand ordered Bron, the artillery chief, to install a weapon on the tower of the church of San Francisco.[43]

While the preparations for the defense were fine-tuned, Ferrand kept open communication with the council of notables of the city, which manifested apprehension in regard to the lack of lodging caused by the high number of refugees.[44]

Confident enough that Dessalines would not prevail, Ferrand wrote to the commander of Samaná, on the eastern part of the island, encouraging him to resist any hostile band that reached there and to obtain useful information: "The brigands are always under the walls, and I have reason to believe that they are more disgusted than us, at a siege that they did not foresee to be so hard."[45]

Intrigued as to how the besiegers provisioned themselves, Ferrand suspected that North American ships were supplying them with provisions, and he sent the ship called *Départment du Nord* to waylay the supplies. He wrote to Officer Dupuy that any North American ship found on the waters near the island loaded with flour or provisions should be forced by the French ship to come to Santo Domingo:

Besides the advantage of doing damage to the blacks, I find in that operation the advantage of supplying the city, and this measure will be added to all the others which I have taken in this regard. As for the rest, for more detailed instructions take the trouble of coming to me during the day with Pagard.[46]

At the end of March, the unexpected arrival of a French squadron that was patrolling the Caribbean, and the ensuing supply of the city, made Dessalines abandon the siege. But still in April, Ferrand considered himself under siege, and he wrote to the minister of marine and colonies:

> Since last 15 Ventose the rebel blacks besiege me in the city of Santo Domingo, with an army of eight thousand men of their best troops, commanded by Clervaux, Christophe, Pétion and Jean Philippe Dan. They are in control of the countryside, and not having any more communications with the outside, I am in consequence limited to the weak means that are concentrated in the city, and to the provisions which reach me from time to time by sea, but which are always proportionally insufficient for my needs.
>
> The precautions which I took at the beginning of the siege of sending away the greatest part of the useless mouths in the city on the ships that were in the port area, have given me the double means of diminishing the consumption of provisions and of not allowing, to the men who were afraid, the hope and the desire of embarking. I will strive to keep myself in the city with the means which I have and those which Admiral Missiessy and General Lagrange had the kindness to furnish me with, to their great credit. With the arrival of the reinforcement of 550 men which Your Excellency had the kindness to send me, my forces number 800 regulars and around 1500 men of the Spanish militia, who lack discipline and resolution, the majority composed of blacks, with whom one cannot undertake any risks nor anything decisive. My losses after the siege by the enemy's fire amount to some fifty men. I have more than sixty wounded in the hospitals.[47]

That same day, Ferrand wrote to Vice Admiral Missiessy, thanking him for his help and asking him to go over the southern coast of the island as if he were going to attack the rebels' zone. "That would make the brigands who are in front of the city think, and would suffice to make them raise the siege."[48] On the following day, Ferrand instructed Pichot that two groups of fifteen dragoons each reconnoiter the roads to Azúa and Santiago and that another detachment visit the Galande hacienda.[49]

Ferrand would repeatedly cite the victory in the Santo Domingo siege as the most evident achievement of his command. He would also remember the difficulties and the obstacles imposed by subordinate officials of Governor Toribio de Montes of Puerto Rico against his efforts in defending Santo Domingo.[50]

Ferrand relayed the news of Dessalines's assassination to the Ministry of Marine in October 1806.[51] The Haitian forces divided; General Alexandre Pétion had the allegiance of the south, but Henri Christophe held power in the north. Thinking that it would be more preferable to the British government, which he courted, to set up a monarchical government, Christophe proclaimed himself emperor. His principal base of power was Cap Haitien, and he fostered the exploitation of large plantations. Pétion, on the other hand, parceled out the former estates among his soldiers, to assure himself of a loyal militia.[52] With the Haitian forces divided, the French experienced much less pressure on the western borders of Santo Domingo.

Discipline Problems in the French Army

When Gilbert Guillermin tried to evaluate the reasons for the French defeat at Palo Hincado in 1808, he ascribed the greatest responsibility to Ferrand's lassitude in imposing military discipline. Soldiers had lost familiarity with the requirements of their profession, and the easy Caribbean climate had made them less resistant to the rigors of marches and combat. Curiously, Guillermin's assessment has been repeated without further questioning by some of the later chroniclers. Perhaps one should recall the enmity between the Guillermin family and Ferrand. One of the members of that family was sent packing to Guadeloupe by Ferrand for "agitating the peace of those of us who are zealous in Santo Domingo."[53]

Ferrand's correspondence with his subordinates shows a different view. Ferrand was constantly hovering over the troops' needs. As soon as he arrived in Santo Domingo, he worried that the quarters assigned to the Polish soldiers were too small, and he asked Dubarquier, the commander of the local garrison, to find them a better location.[54]

The recurrent problem of providing enough shirts and shoes is a subject of frequent communication with his adjutant Vives.[55] He was also concerned about the lack of tobacco and of money in the pockets of the troops. He prompted the search for sufficient hammocks for the quarters and for the replacement of inadequate clothing. When reinforcements arrived, Ferrand sought to have them provided with whatever they needed.

In 1806, there was the case of a cavalry sergeant of the Eighty-ninth Half-Brigade who was tried in military court for fighting. Ferrand used the occasion to emit an *ordre du jour*, in which he ratified the military verdict:

> So long as the General understands that there is subordination of inferiors to their superiors, he demands observance from the part of these towards their subordinates, and he will punish equally the faults that arise in the different instances. The General is informed that there are often fights among the military, and he is not ignorant of the fact that these fights are almost always the effect of drunkenness. He recommends more sobriety, and warns that he will severely punish the fighters. The General does not pretend that soldiers live like Capuchins, but it is possible to have diversion without fighting.[56]

Part of the disciplinary problems was the result of the prolonged deployment of troops that had arrived on the island with General Leclerc for the Saint-Domingue campaign, and the boredom of a garrison life which offered little variety.

With the intention of providing alternatives for recreation, Ferrand sponsored a group of military amateurs who wanted to form a theatrical association. Ferrand obtained from the episcopal vicar permission to use the church of Reina, "where everything that had something holy had been destroyed, and which could be regarded as a private building."[57] He also obtained for them the wood necessary for creating scenography.

When the British squadron defeated a French one that was trying to supply Santo Domingo in January 1806, Ferrand tried to rescue the shipwrecked and the survivors to integrate them into his forces. He also signaled that some of the French sailors sought to desert to Puerto Rico, through Samaná Bay, and gave instructions to have them detained.[58]

CHAPTER 4

Thinking of Santo Domingo as a French Colony

Hacienda near Santo Domingo in the nineteenth century.

From the beginnings of his administration, Ferrand showed his inclination to configure the Spanish part of the island as a new French colony. The interval between 1795, when the Treaty of Basel was signed, and 1803 had been ruinous for Santo Domingo. Tens of thousands of people had migrated to Santiago de Cuba, Puerto Rico, Caracas, the United States, and other parts, and they withdrew capital wealth from the Spanish zone. As it was difficult for the migrants to sell their lands, the part of their wealth that was considered more liquid were the slaves, who would always have a market outlet in other countries. In 1801, Toussaint L'Ouverture rushed the occupation of the capital in order to forestall the continuous extraction of slaves who would become free under the prevailing French legislation,[1] but migration continued under Kerversau and Ferrand. The registry of passports for migrants allows us to observe the strong proportion of slaves who figured as legal migrants.

Ferrand tried to stop the emigration of Spaniards, but while political disorder prevailed in the Cibao and the western part of the colony, it was difficult to dissuade those who wanted to leave. But emigration was regulated. It was necessary to obtain a passport and one could only leave through the capital.[2] When an American brig at Puerto Plata attempted to pick up families trying to migrate from the Cibao, the ship was seized and taken to Samaná to be considered a legitimate prize of war.[3]

The case of François Espaillat shows the prevailing dynamic in the initial years of Ferrand's rule. Espaillat was a physician, born in Cahors, in the French Midi, who had been living for many years in the Spanish part of the island. He became a Spanish subject in 1787, married twice, had plenty of land and was a prominent figure in Santiago.[4] At the beginning of 1804, Ferrand had written to urge him to dissuade his neighbors from paying taxes to Dessalines:

> Compare the yoke under which you live to French moderation, and you will not hesitate to send to Santo Domingo officials with whom I will consult, to pull you out from Dessalines's tyranny. That brigand's position and ours at Santo Domingo cannot leave you a moment of uncertainty.[5]

The letter ended with a personal exhortation to Espaillat to abandon such an ambiguous conduct. A month later, Ferrand advised him that he was sending him a passport for him and his family:

> I will see with . . . pleasure that you will use it to abandon the places where honor forbids you to reside, until further notice.[6]

When finally Espaillat was ready to set out for Puerto Rico, Ferrand wrote a letter to the English captain Mudge, head of the British squadron that patrolled the waters of Santo Domingo:

> I take the liberty of particularly recommending to you M. Espaillat's family, which embarks today to pass to Puerto Rico. This family, as well as those who are on the same ship, have

been forced to abandon their property, and that which they bear on them amounts to their whole fortune. It is for you to say, dear commander, that they are entitled to your sense of humanity, and I am convinced, if chance puts these migrants under your power that you will treat them as favorably as so many people that do not cease to praise you.[7]

Espaillat died in Aguadilla, Puerto Rico, in 1807, but his sons and grandchildren returned to Santo Domingo.[8]

By means of proclamations printed in different Caribbean urban centers, Ferrand sought the return of those who had migrated. He promised the return of their properties and the protection of the authorities. Apparently very few returned, even after Ferrand warned the absent who had left without passports that their properties would be confiscated.[9]

He also tried to attract the white French migrants from Saint-Domingue who had settled in the Oriente region of Cuba, in Puerto Rico, and in other parts to return to the island and try again to raise their fortunes. To these he promised generous concessions of land and means by which they could acquire laborers.

Citizens, you lack all manner of resources, and the part of the island of Saint-Domingue occupied by the French offers you new ones. Come back to the Island whose advantages you know, and which you cannot consider anything else than your homeland (*patrie*). It is at Santo Domingo where you are expected. You will be provided with lodgings and provisioning for men in condition to bear arms, who establish themselves in Santo Domingo. All people who would inhabit the countryside would find there the means of existence. They will be lodged by the Government, as conveniently as possible. To those people who would be willing to live in the countryside, facilities would be extended. They would not have anything else to do but to seed and plant, to obtain benefits beyond their needs. They will have from the Government all the facilities which they might want. The governments of the neighboring colonies have been invited by us in the name of the French Government to seek out for the former inhabitants of Saint-Domingue the means with which to arrive in Santo Domingo. Citizens, I desire that you will not have to fear similar events to those which forced you to aban-

don the Island of Saint-Domingue, and you will be in condition
to expect that France, after having re-established tranquility in
this island, will put you back in possession of your properties.
You will live under a paternal government, in a country where
provisions exist in abundance and where confidence makes
progress every day.[10]

As a propaganda document, the proclamation isn't lacking in
interest. Addressed only to white Frenchmen, it simultaneously eras-
es a stormy past and promises a bountiful future under a paternal
government. The fact that men of age to bear arms are mentioned
has the effect of evoking the latent menace of the rebels in the western part of the island. Although the sense of security is not bolstered,
confidence in the institutions is promoted.

At least in the Samaná peninsula, Ferrand was able to assemble a
number of French settlers, many of them former landholders in
Saint-Domingue or French army officers who planned to establish
themselves on the island.

One of these officials was Ferrand himself. At the beginning of
1808, he bought a property in Samaná to establish a coffee hacienda.[11] One of his subordinates, who had experience in Saint-
Domingue, explained to him in detail all the operations that must be
carried out in order for a coffee hacienda to flourish.

How to Set Up a Coffee Hacienda

Lieutenant Castel la Boulbène, the subordinate who detailed for
Ferrand the steps to be taken to establish a coffee hacienda, first considered the expense of stripping away undesired vegetation in the
160 *tareas* of land that Ferrand wanted to plant.[12] Castel said that this
chore, to be done by "Spaniards," would cost three *gourdes* for every
tarea. A lower price could have been obtained, if it did not include
the burning of the trees that need to be destroyed, but since that
operation had to be undertaken in any case, it was better to contract
the whole operation with the same people. Only haciendas that were
already established could afford to delegate this work to some slaves,

when they had nothing else to do. But it was impossible that someone who started operations with five slaves, including a female who was in lactation, and who had so much to do would undertake such a considerable amount of tree cutting. It as inadvisable to make these small economies until one could maintain the slaves with a henhouse, a fruit orchard or vegetable plot, and a planting of bananas as well as a house and a meadow for the cattle.

At the beginning, said Castel, one must build a modest house until one was able to choose the best woods to construct the definitive one. That first house was made to last six or seven years. In this region, which was very humid, it was convenient to make a quality palisade, with palm tree boards, to last four or five years. In any case, the first place one chose to build would be replaced in the long run by a better location that appeared when all the land had been cleared. For that reason, it was advisable to be moderate in the initial construction expenses, because they were regarded almost as lost deposits. However, in his visit to Ferrand's land, Castel had seen a hill ten minutes from the San Juan River that had a magnificent view over the lands where the planting of coffee trees would begin. In case Ferrand was thinking of building there, and even if the house seemed to have been designed too large, Castel recommended adding a porch on the southern side, which would help the ventilation of the house and would make it healthier. He was aware of only two houses in Samaná that lacked a porch.

He urged General Ferrand to send to M. Bernis as soon as possible the necessary tools, which were not available in Samaná. For each slave an ax should be sent, and the so-called Catalans were the best. Also each slave should be provided with a *manchete* (machete) made by Dampierre, and not by Romero, "who makes detestable ones." Also needed were rakes, hoes, pruning cutters, and other implements. "That is, my General, the complete equipment which you should send to each one of your five slaves, and with it you should equip each one of those you send afterward. And as infallibly happens that ever some tool is broken or lost, it would be well that the hacienda's warehouses had a replacement, to avoid the loss of time."

Castel listed other useful tools and implements. He also mentioned the difficulty of obtaining beasts of burden in Samaná. He recommended that a good horse and a mule be sent from Santo Domingo. He affirmed that donkeys have difficulty in maneuvering through the underbrush and that they were not strong enough to bring provisions for a whole week from town in a single trip. It would also be expedient to send horse apparel from Santo Domingo, because it is not made in Samaná.

It was important, continued Canel, to appoint someone trustworthy as administrator, who had access to four or five hundred *gourdes* to pay the workers and the purveyors of goods. "This precaution," he noted, "is indispensable in Samaná, where the workers' population is almost all foreign, and also extremely distrustful." They had to be paid in cash as soon as their labor was done. "If a single time one makes them wait, that will suffice for them to develop aversion to an hacienda," so that they would not want to return to work there. It was essential with such people to develop a reputation for prompt payment, and the only way to achieve it was to deposit money with someone of trust.

Samaná merchants neither wanted nor were able to extend credit. Government funds were so tight that no one counted on them. In a postscript, Castel added that among the drugs Ferrand should send Bernis, he should include a strong dose of *alcali volatile flux*, which was the only effective remedy against the bite of the extremely large scorpions peculiar to the region. "Slaves may be bitten while they work in the woods, and without this *alcalí* they inevitably die".

The Problem of Labor

It is interesting to note in Castel's communication his confidence that Ferrand would be able to increase the number of slaves at his disposal and, at the same time, his conviction that skilled labor must be contracted in order that efforts at the planned hacienda go forward. For those who still recalled the extraordinary productivity of Saint-Domingue before the revolution, slave labor seemed to be an indispensable component of any profitable economic enterprise. The same conviction was found then in all the Caribbean islands. A world without slaves was inconceivable. Nevertheless, by the date Castel was writing to Ferrand, Great Britain had already decided to abolish the slave trade from Africa. To us it seems evident, in retrospective, that in a colony that neighbored the new republic of Haiti, it was naive to think that slavery could flourish again.

The disposition of captured slaves in ships taken by the privateers sparked great interest among the French settled in Santo Domingo. When the slave ship was stranded on the Higuey coast at the beginning of 1804, Ferrand's solicitude was to prevent landowners from appropriating the slaves without paying the treasury for them.[13] In subsequent captures, it was noticeable that the priciest items were the slaves.

The Marketing of Production

The lack of sufficient labor was not the only obstacle preventing Santo Domingo from becoming a profitable colony for France. While the war with Great Britain lasted, the recurrence of the British blockade frustrated the attempts to market its products. French ships and those of its allies were vulnerable to interception. North Americans came largely for the mahogany logging, for which Ferrand granted licenses.[14] What could be done in wartime with the sugar and the coffee that was produced?

On March 2, 1808, Ferrand wrote to Admiral Daures, commander of the British forces in Jamaica, on the occasion of sending to Jamaica a Reverend Hamilton and his family, who had been captured by a privateer. The schooner on which he sent Hamilton was loaded with mahogany and belonged to Alexandre Gazan, a French trader established in Santo Domingo. Gazan was charged with liquidating the letters of change that Hamilton had given to recover the objects taken by the privateer. To pay for the expenses for the trip to Jamaica, Gazan carried the shipment of mahogany, with whose sale and Hamilton's payment Gazan expected to acquire in Kingston necessary goods for Santo Domingo. Ferrand's striking expressions merit replication here:

As M. Gazan is one of the heads of a well-esteemed commercial house, he intends, under Your Excellency's protection, to manage a commercial link between Jamaica and Santo Domingo. This reciprocal movement would facilitate the exchange of objects we need, with the cattle, *mahogany* and logwood and other goods that we can furnish the reciprocal trade, with the express restriction, however, of the articles that our state of war prohibits. Persuaded in advance, M. the Admiral, that Your Excellency will not find any inconvenience for such relations, I have trusted M. Gazan with a certain sum in letters of exchange, on the United States of America, which he is commissioned to use, according to the approval you may give to the project that I have the honor to present to you. Our position in the colonies is different from that in Europe, and our common advantage makes a rule of relaxing that national animosity which Fate has exalted so strongly. It is allowed to us, without compromising our responsibility, to hand ourselves to arrangements and to the promotion of the natural esteem whose convenience war should never interdict. The friendly correspondence that you have wanted to maintain with me, makes me believe that Your Excellency will share a way of seeing and principles that do not hurt our honor in anything or the interests of our sovereigns.[15]

Ferrand's bold proposal of trade did not have a sequel, but it shows an active imagination that seeks to find a way out of a deadlock in which the rivalry of Great Britain and France had obstructed his project of turning Santo Domingo into a prosperous colony.

French Institutions in Santo Domingo

The process of turning Santo Domingo into an annex, first of the French Republic and afterward of the empire, was already under way when Ferrand took the reins of power in December 1803. The Spanish part of the island had been divided into the Ozama and Cibao departments, and these were in turn divided in districts (*arrondissements*) that grouped the twenty-four communes in which the former *partidos* had been gathered.

The capital had its own municipal council, in which Ferrand had insisted that there be representation both of the "Spaniards" and of the French. Under Ferrand's pressure, the council published an ordinance for the cleanliness and sanitation of the streets. It was written both in French and in Spanish. Its first article read: "Streets will be swept regularly at seven in the morning, and trash will be carried to the seashore."[16]

Another of Ferrand's concerns was the exactitude of weights and measures.[17] The French Republican calendar was in force until the beginning of 1806, when the old Gregorian calendar was reinstated in France.

In 1806, the *Calendrier Historique et Statistique de l'Ile de Saint-Domingue* was published in Paris.[18] An interesting section on the judicial branch detailed the hybrid arrangements by which the courts now functioned in the colony, especially at the local level. In previous Spanish practice, the local mayor acted as a judge of small claims and petty cases. In such cases, the mayor would have the advice of lawyers, notaries, and local experts, but many of these persons had migrated. What was done was to abridge the mayors' jurisdiction in such cases and facilitate the appeals. The immediate appeals courts were constituted with both French and Spanish members, and cases were adjudicated according to the law of the litigants, according to the old Roman maxim, operating in the ancien régime courts in France, *actio sequitur forum rei* (i.e., the legal action follows the jurisdiction to which the matter in question belongs). Perhaps Ferrand was harking back to his Besançon youth, because in the Franche Comté, annexed to France in the seventeenth century, different civil codes and procedures had coexisted before the revolution.[19] The ultimate appeals court was similarly composed of French and Spanish members. Like the old Spanish *audiencia*, it had the captain general as its presiding officer. The Spanish members were ecclesiastics: the vicar general, Pedro Prado; the pastor of Santa Bárbara, Jose Ruiz; and the cathedral pastor, Bernardo Correa.[20]

In April 1808, Ferrand commissioned a M. Palomine the translation of the French Civil Code into Spanish, "to make it known and to have it observed in the different *arrondissements* of the departments of the Ozama and the Cibao."[21]

By Ferrand's instructions, the referendum to ratify the transition from the republic to the empire was carried out. In 1808, Ferrand encouraged the celebration of the feast of Saint Napoleon on the fifteenth of August, the emperor's birthday, by giving clothing to the indigent.[22] It is hard to discern whether Ferrand was enthusiastic about the new imperial regime in France.

But although Ferrand in a large measure implemented the French institutions in Santo Domingo, he modified it in two significant aspects. On account of disagreements on fiscal matters, he entered into a jurisdictional conflict with the previously appointed departmental prefect, whom he sent back to France. The Ministry of Colonies finally prevailed in puttin fiscal checks in place over Ferrand's administration. Again, for supposed restraints to his executive powers, Ferrand suspended the Tribunal of First Recourse and replaced it with a judicial commission.[23]

The Uneasy Cohabitation
of French and Dominicans

Early in Ferrand's administration in Santo Domingo, the administrator of ecclesiastical properties, a holdover from the Spanish regime named González, supposedly said in front of ten people at the Michel hacienda near Montegrande that so long as the French had few troops, they would be amiable toward the local inhabitants, but that things would change when reinforcements came. As for him, he had his reserves in Puerto Rico and would depart to there when more French troops arrived, and he was surprised that the Spaniards could complain about Toussaint's previous rule.[24] On hearing of this, Ferrand had González arrested, deposed from his office, and sent out of the island.

Ferrand's efforts to assimilate Santo Domingo to the French regime encountered considerable obstacles, not only in the Dominicans' natural resistance to the imposition of a language, institutions, and customs alien to their tradition but also on account of the inability of Ferrand and his officials to overcome their own bias.

An important element in their differences was the racialism with which the French tinged the institutions they sponsored. In repeated communications to his subordinates, Ferrand, who was unable to overcome the trauma of the defeat inflicted on the French by the Haitian insurgents, let his deep hatred and contempt for the blacks, especially the Haitians, shine through. Although he promoted the founding of schools in the colony, he expressly excluded from them the sons of blacks, because their destiny was to work in the fields, for which they did not need schooling. He tenaciously opposed marriage between whites and blacks, and one occasion he demanded that a parish priest annul an interracial marriage that the latter had performed. He measured the quality of the population he governed by the proportion of people of color in it.

Another source of differences was the element of religion. Although Ferrand was conscientious in allowing public Catholic worship, he did not show much patience with popular religious expression. On May 18, 1808, he wrote to his subordinate Pichot:

> I noticed that yesterday evening Spanish black men and women ran on the streets at nine and a half, taking along with them French slaves and singing and making a tumult contrary to good order. They take as pretext night ceremonies, which they call stations, which cannot be approved either by the Church or the government, because under the guise of devotion they occasion the greatest disorders. Would you take care in consequence to give orders that such gatherings do not take place, and that individuals of that sort that may be found on the streets after the prescribed hour be arrested.[25]

Two days later, he wrote again to Pichot:

> A delegation of devotees has just made me a request to celebrate, at Santa Bárbara, the feasts in honor of the Holy Ghost. I have put in a recommendation to their petition that I allow them to celebrate it in the church, from four in the morning until nine in the evening, and that outside those hours the church must be closed. I have also permitted all the processions, stations, rosaries, etc., during the day, until the hour of closing. If they deviate from this order, have them arrested.[26]

On the eve of the feast of Saint John the Baptist the same year, he wrote to Pichot that he was not opposed to the celebration of the feast or the horseback riding in the city, but he asked vigilance to avoid the accidents that horse races usually occasion, and he insisted that the diversion end at the appointed time. Free people galloping through the city must be arrested and taken to the guardhouse on the square, from which they would not be released until a fine of five *gourdes* be paid. In the case of slaves arrested for the same transgression, they were to be lashed twenty-five times.[27]

His relationship with the Catholic hierarchy was not exempt from ironies. The first prelate with whom Ferrand dealt was Murviel, a bishop of the French Constitutional Church, sent in mission by a synod of that church to become pastor of the faithful in Saint-Domingue. When the French were expelled from Saint-Domingue, Murviel moved to Santo Domingo, where he had himself acknowledged as the ordinary by the few members of the clergy who had remained in the Spanish part of the island. But when the concordat between Napoleon and Pope Pius VII omitted producing a bishop for the Santo Domingo See, the Grand Vicar Prado wrote to Ferrand claiming that Murviel was not the legitimate bishop of the diocese. When Ferrand ascertained that the only mandate that Murviel had was that of the synod of the Constitutional Church, he ordered him to leave the island.[28] Although a Catholic bishop was provided, Ferrand recognized Vicar Prado as the Catholic Church's representative and garnered his loyalty by vague promises of recommending him for the miter.

Prado was useful in keeping the few priests loyal to Ferrand, who used the parish pastors to mobilize landowners against the Haitians. After the concordat, he ensured the payment of their salaries. But in 1808, with the situation drastically changing in Europe, the entente between the French administration and the Catholic clergy became brittle.

Civil Marriages in Santo Domingo under Ferrand

The French colonial administration since the time of Louis XIV kept the practice of making duplicate books of baptisms, marriages, and burials so that in case of hurricanes or other disasters, there would be a copy in France of the parish registers—so vital in pre-revolutionary France for the civil documentation on individuals. When the revolution instituted the use of civil records in place of the parish registers, the practice of sending duplicates to France was continued. For that reason, there is a copy in Aix-en-Provence of the civil records of Santo Domingo under the French occupation, and these in turn have been microfilmed to make them accessible in the National Archives.

Of particular interest are the marriage records. Although there are only 58 marriages recorded for the period 1801 to 1806,[29] one must remember that the population of the city of Santo Domingo was small at the time and that most of the marital unions outside the city were not recorded in the available French civil records. Of the 58 marriages recorded, 37 (almost two-thirds of the total) were between people born in Santo Domingo, most of them born in the city or in its neighboring communities. In addition, there was one marriage between two free black persons—the man born in an hacienda in Haina and the woman born in Guinea, a widow and resident of the same hacienda[30]—and a marriage between a slave, Pierre Joseph Gusman, born on the island, and a free black woman, María Polonia Sánchez, both residents of the city.[31]

Of marriages between French people born in Saint-Domingue there were four, and between Frenchmen born in France and women born in French Saint-Domingue there were three. Four Frenchmen married women born in Santo Domingo, and two couples were of French-born consorts. One Frenchman married a woman born in the Canary Islands. Five other combinations also appear, all involving a man born outside the island marrying a Dominican woman: a Spaniard, an Italian, a Savoyard, a native of Costa Firme (Venezuela), and a Pole. The Italian, the Savoyard, and the Pole, as well as several of the French men belonged to the French army.

The professions of those marrying as well as those of the witnesses to the ceremony showed a wide array of craftsmen. Many of these professions were linked to the services essential to the garrison.

The Census of January 1, 1808

Population estimates of Spanish Santo Domingo around 1800 ranged from 120,000 to 135,000 inhabitants, of which around 15,000 were slaves.[32] As a result of war and emigration, the number of inhabitants went down in the following years.

The best representation of the Spanish part of the island under French administration is provided by the census of population and production of January 1, 1808.[33] The eighteen communes of the department of Ozama and the six communes of the department of Cibao showed a total population ascending to 50,089 persons, of whom 43,037 were free and 7,052 were slaves. The proportion of slaves (14 percent) was remarkably strong, when on the neighboring island of Puerto Rico slaves still did not reach 11 percent. In spite of the economic crisis resulting from the emigration of so many Dominicans with their capital resources and the British blockade of commercial vessels, there was a strong contingent of labor available for landowners.

The capital, Santo Domingo, reported 6,029 free people and 1,169 slaves, for a total of 7,198 inhabitants. In spite of being in the forefront of the French war against the Haitian insurgents and the emigration of many local inhabitants, Santiago de los Caballeros surpassed the capital in population, with 7,524 free people and 1,304 slaves, a total of 8,828 persons. These numbers mean that almost a third of the population was located in the two principal centers of population. The third-ranking commune was La Vega, also in the department of Cibao, with 5,548 inhabitants. El Seybo only had 3,510 persons, and Ingenios accounted for 2,869 free people and 372 slaves. No other commune reached 3,000 inhabitants.

In addition to its division by civil condition, the population was counted by the categories of white Europeans, native whites, Creoles of color, and slaves, and it was also counted by the number of men, women, and children. It is evident that the majority of white Europeans was concentrated in the capital. In the city of Santo Domingo, there were more native white women (1,113) than men of the same denomination (491). The Creoles of color dominated in number in El Seybo, Ozama, Higuey, Bayaguana, Monte Grande, Llanos, Isabela, Ingenios, Baní, Azúa, Neyba, La Vega, Cotuí, and Puerto Plata. The only commune in which the number of slaves approached that of the free was Samaná (279 slaves and 306 free persons).

Children made up a great proportion of the population, and it is interesting to see from this category that slaves, although in lesser proportion than the free, were having offspring. For instance, in Baní, 128 men and 101 women slaves had 78 children among them; and in Ingenios, there were 165 men and 121 women slaves with 79 children. In other communes, the proportion was weaker. In Monte Grande, there were only 10 children for 90 male and 70 female slaves.

It is obvious that the communes farthest removed from the rebel contingents showed higher populations. In a note to the census, this explanation was offered:

> One will find the reason for it in the disasters which have befallen all the communes bordering the former French part, the most populaous and the richest, such as Saint-Raphael, Saint-Michel, Hincha, Banico, Las Cahovas, La Mata, Saint-Jean, Neyba, as well as . . . Monte Christ, in the department of Cibao. The numerous families of these parishes which have escaped the blades of the rebel murderers have almost all perished by the deplorable sequels of discouragement from misery and from adversities.[34]

There were communes that reported few inhabitants, such as Bollar (170 persons), but generally in the Spanish part of the island one notices a higher population that the repeated reports of depopulation would have made one expect. The proportion of the young population points to a rapid recuperation. The notes on the population census end with a positive note on Samaná:

> The population will grow, and it would flow most notably to Samaná, by reason of the . . . the happy combination of maritime

trade and colonial cultivations [in] which the geographical situation and the new establishments that have been made on this peninsula promise progress for the metropolis.[35]

The census also included figures of production grouped by communes.[36] Coffee was the principal crop, and its production was concentrated in the department of Cibao. Of a total of 1,138,271 coffee trees, 875,533 were in the jurisdictions of Santiago, La Vega, Cotuí, Puerto Plata, Moca, and Samaná. Although the total number of coffee trees may look impressive, if we calculate an average of 800 trees an acre, the total would be equivalent to some 1,425 acres planted in coffee.

There were only 8,506 *carreaux* of sugarcane planted, 5,804 of them in the department of Ozama. There were 19,304 cotton plants, most of which (17,869) were in the department of Ozama, especially in Isabela and El Seybo. Cacao (95,883 trees) was concentrated in Ingenios (77,100 trees). Tobacco was reduced to 2,331 *carreaux*, of which 1,580 lay in Santiago.

Cattle amounted to 49,745 head, two-thirds of which were in the Ozama department, especially in El Seybo, Llanos, and Monteplata. In the department of Cibao, the principal cattle raisers were La Vega and Cotuí. There was a total of 371 sheep, of which 150 were reported in Baní. Of 48,000 pigs there were more than 15,000 in La Vega and more than 8,000 in Santiago.

Viability of Santo Domingo as a French Colony

If the events of 1808 had not dictated the contrary, would Santo Domingo have developed as a French colony? The census data seem to indicate that possibility. Compared with other jurisdictions that at the time changed metropolis, like Mauritius, Saint Lucia, Florida, and Louisiana, the Spanish part of the island the French called Saint-Domingue could have had the same possibilities for growth as a prosperous colony under new rule without losing its language, like Saint Lucia, or its institutions, like Louisiana.[37] But it would not have been easy: economic forces alone do not shape the history of a people.

Ferrand and
the Events of 1808

General Marie-Louis Ferrand.

In 1807, with the Peace of Tilsit, the Napoleonic Empire was at the height of its power. It was true that Great Britain ruled the seas and that France had seen most of its overseas colonies occupied, but French armies moved freely in Europe, and almost all of those zones of Europe that were not allied with Napoleon were occupied by his armies. After the meeting between Alexander I of Russia and Napoleon, one could expect that negotiations would start between Great Britain and France to create the conditions for a lasting peace.

That, however, does not seem to have been in Napoleon's plans.

The attempt to ruin British trade by means of the imposition of the Continental System; the desire to occupy Portugal, which refused to cut its historic commercial links with Great Britain; and above all, the precipitated occupation of Spain and the displacement of the Spanish royal family made 1808 the year in which the Napoleonic Empire began its decline.

When Joachim Murat, brother-in-law of Napoleon and commander in chief of his troops in Spain, advised him in a private letter that the people in Madrid were restless and hostile against the presence of French troops and the impending departure of the rest of the royal family to France, Napoleon answered on April 9, 1808:

> I see that you attach in general too much importance to the opinion of the city of Madrid. I have not gathered the Grande Armée in Spain to follow the fantasies of the populace in Madrid.[1]

A month later the fantasies of the populace of Madrid had unchained the Spanish War of Independence, but Napoleon let some time pass before he took notice. He already thought himself the lord of the Spanish Empire in America. On May 21, he wrote to Murat:

> My brother, I see on the May 16 report of the Ministry of Marine that he fears that Puerto Rico and Havana lack provisions, as a consequence of the embargo put on American shipping. Initially Havana can provision itself through Florida and Puerto Rico by the Spanish continent.[2]

He recommended that letters be written to the respective captains general to have them provide for the planting of potatoes and other crops to reduce the consumption of wheat, as he had already instructed to be done in Martinique.

The Junta of Seville Sends News

Meanwhile authorities in Cuba and Puerto Rico were receiving another kind of communication. The Supreme Junta established in Seville by the insurrectionists against the occupying French sent its version of the May events to the Spanish dominions in America. The Marquis of Someruelos, captain general of Cuba, issued a printed proclamation on July 17, 1808:

Inhabitants of the Island of Cuba, Worthy Sons of the Generous Spanish Nation, Know that I have just received today some manifestos, proclamations and circulars published and printed by order of the Supreme Junta of Government which has been established in Seville as a result of an act of the most infamous perfidy that the centuries has seen or read.[3]

Someruelos proceeded to urge pledges of loyalty to King Ferdinand VII and, in his absence, to the Supreme Junta. He exhorted Cubans to suppress their "inevitable disquiet, so that you will avoid all clamor and disorder, and so that you will abstain from inflicting the slightest vexation on the pacific, laborious and most useful Frenchmen our comrades and friends."

In a second proclamation, on August 8, Someruelos narrated the violence perpetrated by the French in Madrid and other parts of Spain. He then praised "British heroism" and encouraged listeners to contribute to the Spaniards' patriotic efforts:

[S]o I expect that you will rush to subscribe on the sacred tablets of patriotism which by disposition of the Most Illustrious City Council are open in the residences of the councilmen and the Procurador Síndico, the Count of Santa María de Loret, Don Juan Crisóstomo Peñalver y Barreto, and Don Tomás de la Cruz Muñoz, handing in to them the jewels, products and other goods which you may have convenient, and to the General Treasury, quantities of money.[4]

Apparently the first governor to receive the news of the uprising in Spain was the captain general of Puerto Rico, Toribio de Montes, who received emissaries from the Junta on July 14, two days before the governor of Cuba was informed. Together with the bishop of Puerto Rico, Alejo de Arizmendi, and the *cabildo* of the city of San Juan, Montes proceeded to declare his loyalty to Ferdinand VII and to the Supreme Junta. In his proclamation of July 29, he flattered the inhabitants:

Spanish-Puerto Ricans. Too well known is your fidelity and loyalty to the Catholic Kings of Spain ever since Divine Providence put this Island under their empire, and therefore any exhortation is superfluous, or any proclamation to renew in you that loyalty and fidelity which you have preserved and sustained against the greatest attackers of the Spanish Crown who have longed for and without end crave for the possession of this precious island.[5]

Montes accused Napoleon of "pretending to subjugate you to his despotism, dethroning the amiable sovereign whom you have recognized by solemn oath, and to destroy our Holy Religion." This same theme of a menace to religion was seized upon by Bishop Arizmendi, who in a pastoral letter to the faithful exhorted devotion to the sovereign, and he instituted nocturnal prayers in the cathedral to obtain his restitution to the throne. His exhortation implied that Napoleon was redolent of hellish sulfur. The *Gaceta del Gobierno de Puerto-Rico* informed that on the day the government took its oath of loyalty to Ferdinand VII there was popular enthusiasm:

> [O]n the streets only voices of repeated *vivas* and acclamations were heard, and from the lowest class to the most elevated one the rejoicing and mirth which had inspired such a commendable event were demonstrated. . . . The Illustrious Don Juan Alejo de Arizmendi, worthy bishop of this diocese, on that day threw from the balconies of his palace considerable amounts of coin to the People, spurred by the keen zeal which he has ever demonstrated and shown for the greater service of His Majesty and the singular pleasure he had in that pleasant act.[6]

Governor Montes urged all to wear as an emblem a scarlet cockade

> without exception of person, state or condition, on the hat, with this difference, that the militia and the employees who enjoy a salary from the King, must place on the center of the said cockade, another, smaller black one, to signify the armistice and alliance between the Spanish and English nations, and both these and the rest may also add a cipher or the initial letters of the august name of our sovereign Don Ferdinand VII to signify more individually the objects of the emblem. We warn you that after eight days of the publication of this edict those who do not bear it will be considered suspicious, and they would be dealt with according to the law.[7]

It is curious, but one would also say predictable, that in Cuba they thought first about gathering concrete resources and in Puerto Rico about making loyalties visible.

Meanwhile in Santo Domingo, General Ferrand had not received news of the uprising in May in Spain and its effects in neighboring Cuba and Puerto Rico. Confidently he wrote on August 6 to governor Montes recommending Claude Vives, his chief of staff, who would be making a stop in Mayaguez before continuing on his voyage to France. The stop was due to the fact that the schooner *Le Grand* on which he was traveling had not found sufficient coffee to load in Santo Domingo. As he did habitually, Ferrand closed the letter saying: "I will not leave the French government ignorant of all the interest you have placed to hasten and to make successful such an important expedition, and in seconding it by all the means which would be at your disposal."[8] But Vives, who had in 1806 in Santo Domingo married the daughter of a Saint-Domingue refugee,[9] never did arrive in France but would appear later in a list of prisoners of war of the English.[10]

Ferrand first learned of the political change when a schooner from Puerto Rico arrived in Santo Domingo with a letter from Toribio de Montes dated August 2 and carried by Francisco Bracetti. Bracetti had been directed to bring back to Santo Domingo a M. Chevalier, a privateer, with two sailors, and the French agent in Puerto Rico, M. Panel. In his answer to Montes, Ferrand showed astonishment at the war declared against Napoleon by the Junta of Seville:

> I acknowledge that I did not know about the political existence of that Council, or of the character of which it may have been invested to carry out acts that only belong to a legitimate sovereign.[11]

Ferrand declared that notwithstanding what might be happening in Europe, he would continue observing the same conduct as before toward the Spanish. He affirmed that the Spanish in Santo Domingo remained at peace and ready to reject all the suggestions that would alter their union with the French.

In a postscript to Montes, Ferrand complained that Bracetti and

the members of his crew had presented themselves wearing a cockade "which did not seem to me to be the emblem of any legitimate
government legally recognized."[12] He felt called to constrain them
not to wear it in public while they stayed in Santo Domingo.

The War of Letters

Ferrand shared the news he had received with the population by
means of a proclamation on August 9:

> News I have just received from Puerto Rico shows that this
> Spanish colony has delivered itself to a political ferment that
> can produce no other but sinister and deplorable effects. The
> cause of this tempest, which perhaps will perturb all the Spanish
> possessions in America, seems to originate from some move-
> ments of discord and rupture which Fate has moved between
> the French and the Spanish in Europe. Events that show so
> many contradictions, incoherence and counter-sense, that their
> existence and origin are still, before our eyes, wrapped in an
> almost impenetrable obscurity.[13]

Ferrand made an exhortation to preserve harmony between the
French and the Spanish, telling them that they formed one community of brothers and friends "who do not have but the same interest
in defending themselves, the same spirit and the same sentiments."

On August 18, Ferrand instructed the printer to publish in the next
edition of the fortnightly *Bulletin* the correspondence between
Montes and him.[14] Montes again wrote on August 26, and with the
letter he sent the remaining ten sailors from Chevalier's privateer,
seized in the bay of San Juan. In his answer, Ferrand complained
again about Bracetti, who allegedly distributed anti-French propaganda. He added:

> M. Captain-General, the tone, the style of the letters and the
> proclamations that M. Bracetti bears, have made me cognizant
> of the spirit of insurrection that prevails among the inhabitants
> of Puerto Rico. It bears the same character and contains the

same elements that had by degrees conducted the French Revolution to the last period of barbarity and demoralization. I was myself a witness to the storms and the periodic horrors of that revolution, and I have always observed that the weakness of the government had in some way prepared them, by not taking in time the most energetic measures to contain the movements of a disoriented people who no longer knew the brake when they had taken the first step in the path of anarchy and crime and who are ready to overthrow today the idols to which yesterday they offered incense.[15]

Ferrand's warning is interesting, not only for what it reveals of his sentiments toward the period of the Terror in France, when he had been arrested, but also for what it reveals of his efforts to influence Montes's mind. It is obvious that the rejection of the French regime in Madrid has not come from the people in Puerto Rico, but that it has been induced by Montes himself, but Ferrand seems to be telling him that once a people has learned to reject authorities, it could turn against Montes himself. He goes on:

It is as your friend, as a friend of the unhappy inhabitants of Puerto Rico, that I share with you these observations, in which Your Excellency may find some disinterested and perhaps wise advice. Cursed be those who provoke, foment or tolerate revolutions prepared for the insurrection of the People, and if they want to enlighten themselves with an example as instructive as it is terrible, let them read and meditate the fearful annals of the French Revolution, which successively devoured all those who had been the promoters of its excesses and the partisans of its furies.[16]

If all this seems to indicate that Ferrand was trying to rattle Montes, the postscript confirms it:

The news I have received and which cannot be doubted announces that the Supreme Junta of the Spanish Government, the Grandees of Spain, the Deputies of the Clergy, of the Inquisition, of the Council of the Indies, and of the Treasury, as well as the principal cities of the Kingdom, have met at Bayonne, where an Extraordinary Junta has been formed, and they, in the name of their nation, have recognized Joseph Napoleon as King of the Spaniards and of the Indies and they have rendered him an oath of fidelity.

Ferrand suggests that the British have misrepresented the news to Montes, and that the Puerto Ricans would repent of their actions when the truth became established and they found that they had been in rebellion against Spain as well as against the French, their true friends and their loyal allies, and all that to bind themselves to some elements without reputation.

On August 30, Ferrand wrote to Diego Mercedes, the interim commander of El Seybo, who had informed him on a letter of the 26th about incursions on the coast "of the pirates from Puerto Rico and the English." He approved the placement of an observation post on the coast "to prevent the brigandage which the enemy has allowed itself against your commune" and sent him one hundred rounds of ammunition.[17] The supplies were meager, but, as always, the rhetoric was lofty:

> I have seen with pleasure the sincere expressions of your zeal and of your devotion to His Majesty, as well as the proofs of your vigilance for the conservation and the defense of your land. I will be delighted (*charmé*) to recognize your services when the occasion presents itself.

But for Toribio de Montes, the time for correspondence had passed, and there were other elements in the air.

Juan Sánchez Ramírez

According to Gilbert Guillermin's account of the insurrection, published in Philadelphia in 1810, "Puerto Rico, where there prevailed a disquieting ferment, even among the heads of government of the island, would soon become the center of the most Machiavellian machinations imagined by superstition and directed by the influence of a fanatical clergy."[18] Since July, the Dominican refugees in Puerto

Rico had asked Governor Toribio de Montes to attempt a coup in Santo Domingo, for which they offered him fifty thousand *gourdes*. As a result of their efforts, an agent called Sarmiento went to El Seybo to organize the revolt. Agustín Franco, commander of the department of Cibao, notified Ferrand of these plots, but Ferrand did not give any credence to them. According to Guillermin, on September 15, the ship *Juste* brought the approbation of the Junta of Seville to these actions. In charge of undertaking them was Juan Sánchez Ramírez, former commander of Cotuí.

Ferrand's correspondence in the years prior to 1808 reveals a pattern of cordial relations with Sánchez Ramírez.[19] How that relationship unraveled is still unclear. What is certain is that in the summer of 1808, Juan Sánchez Ramírez began to plot a rising against the French. According to a letter he wrote in September 1808, thanks to the efforts of Captain Bracetti, he had learned in Santo Domingo the month before about the Spanish uprising against the French. Whether spurred by migrants and authorities outside the island or impelled by his own political vision, he dedicated himself to organize the revolution. In his own words:

> On the seventh of last month, I came to Santo Domingo, when I found the news of the declaration of war by the Spanish against the French, which captain Bracetti carried, and from that moment I dedicated myself to arousing the will of the native-born Spanish, who were asleep and trusting.[20]

Sánchez Ramírez' efforts were not exempt from mishaps, because he found out that some people were "passionately in favor of the French and others satisfied with them." But he told his correspondents, the priests Isidoro Ximinian y Pela and Juan Antonio Pichardo, vicars of the parish of Mayaguez in Puerto Rico, in September 1808:

> Believe me that without thinking more in this important business, I do not omit a step nor do I avoid inconvenience, nor do I fear danger, until I see the Spanish flag flying in Santo Domingo, and we with glad voices joyfully shout, *Viva Ferdinand VII, Our Emperor and August King.*[21]

In a petition to the viceroy of New Spain, dated August 28, 1809, Sánchez Ramírez affirmed that in 1808 he received twenty thousand pesos from the commanding general of the marine in La Habana and several small remittances in provisions and money from the governor of Puerto Rico.[22] In their communications to the Junta of Seville in November 1808, both Sánchez Ramírez and Montes indicated that in October 1808, Montes sent him three hundred muskets, the corresponding munitions, and other supplies in a brig and a schooner escorted by a British frigate, for fear of French privateers at Samaná. According to a subsequent communication of three Dominican emigrants to the Junta in Seville, Montes required a bond of eighteen thousand pesos, in case the weapons were lost.[23]

Ferrand showed that he was informed of Sánchez Ramírez' activities. In a communication to the military commander of the notables of El Seybo, Ferrand wrote on October 10, 1808:

> I have been informed that false news is circulating in the department of the Cibao, which is said to have been generated by Don Juan Sánchez. That news, which affirms that the Governor of Puerto Rico has sent arms and munitions to the coast of Higuey, which Don Juan Sánchez is charged with receiving, has already reached the inhabitants of this commune which are ready to rebel at his earliest orders, that the parish of Seybo is in the same disposition, etc. Although I do not give any credence to such tales and although I count with the greatest confidence in the inhabitants of El Seybo, it is nonetheless true that there are malicious people who quietly spread this contrived news, without those who should watch over their actions taking care of suppressing it.[24]

On the same date, Ferrand wrote in similar terms to the notables of Higuey:

> Gentlemen, by news to which I am repugnant to give credence, I have been informed that Don Juan Sánchez, of whom I already had told you when it was a question of Sarmiento, maintains relations with the seditious people in Puerto Rico. It is said that he has received weapons, munitions, etc., and that in letters that he has written he assures that he can count on all the

inhabitants of the East for a coup, and that no longer are there Frenchmen in your district. It is necessary that Don Juan Sánchez come to apologize or that two Notables from your district, a Spaniard and a Frenchman, come here, before the 20th of the month, to deny those rumors.[25]

The efforts of other figures implicated in the uprising are not signaled in Ferrand's correspondence, but Guillermin mentions Ciriaco Ramírez, from Azúa; Manuel Ximenez; and Morillo, the pastor of Santiago.[26]

Christophe's Proclamation

In Haiti, the rulers were aware of the situation that was developing on the other part of the island. On September 19, Henri Christophe, President and Generalissimo of the Forces of Land and Sea of the State of Haiti, published a proclamation to "the Spanish inhabitants of the eastern part of the island of Haiti." He drew their attention to the events in Europe and warned them of the designs of the French:

It pertains to you only to assume the attitude of a valiant people and to undo the weak strings by which you remain unconsciously detained. Remember also the former relations with us, inhabitants of the same territory, subject to the same needs. You must see in us natural friends, to whom an identical interest should unite forever.[27]

Christophe offered free access to the markets of his territory, under the most complete security. "I do not assign any particular place to establish the interchanges. Full of confidence in the word which sometime ago you had given me, I will even receive you in the capital of this state."

Toribio de Montes Requests Permission

In Puerto Rico, Toribio de Montes was arming an expedition against the French in Santo Domingo, and when he was near the date of the expedition's departure he requested permission from the Junta in Seville, which surely would not receive the letter until the events were out of its control. On October 15, 1808, Montes wrote to Francisco Saavedra, president of the Junta:

> The part of the island of Santo Domingo that belonged to Spain finds itself with scant hope of help, according to the information which repeatedly its inhabitants, almost all of whom are Spaniards, have manifested to me, and they have assured me that this is the most opportune occasion for its return to the Crown; since they consider and offer to carry it out without the shedding of blood, and at little expense, I had no inconvenience, given the repeated requests that those inhabitants have made to me, in granting them the help of a hired brig and a schooner, and two gunboats belonging to this garrison. All the boats are well armed to carry over four hundred muskets with their bayonets and cartridge belts, two hundred sabers, the corresponding munitions, and two hundred volunteers who have asked me, most of them emigrants from that island, having as their head Don Juan Sánchez Ramírez, one of the richest, most well-off, and well-respected Spanish inhabitants. They have undertaken the obligation to answer with credits against the Royal Treasury of the expenses that arise in the expedition, if Supreme Junta does not approve that it be undertaken by His Majesty's account, or if it does not have the happy success that generally is expected.[28]

Montes suggested that if Spain sent two war frigates with six hundred troops, victory would more easily be achieved, especially if the frigates and six additional gunboats blocked the port of Santo Domingo. He cautioned that the support of the Haitians must not be sought: "I have manifested to them that in no wise should they admit or use their persons, nor those of any nation." He added:

> The twentieth of this month the said expedition will leave this port, and in two days it may cast anchor at Yuma, which has

been chosen and agreed upon for the landing on that Island, and these forces will be commanded by the royal frigate lieutenant Don Martin Espino, to whom I have given the suitable instructions, for he should retire from those coasts after he hands to the aforesaid Sánchez Ramírez what has been sent to him and he has solicited. I hope that my acceptance and determination meets the approval of Your Highness. I have been spurred by the desire of those neighboring Spaniards, [and] the proclamation of General Ferrand that offends the sons of this Island and the whole nation.

Actually the flotilla did not depart from the capital of Puerto Rico until the 22nd. It arrived in Mayaguez the 24th, and it reached the mouth of the Yuma River on the 27th.

The Action Begins

The rebels struck first in El Seybo where, on October 25, Manuel Carvajal arrested the Spanish-born commander Manuel Peralta, who was the principal figure in the area. As had been agreed, Sánchez Ramírez and his followers met the flotilla from Puerto Rico in the port of Yuma, where they offloaded the war supplies and began to transport them on horseback in the direction of El Seybo.

On October 29, Ferrand wrote to Castel, his subordinate in Samaná:

I have been informed that the Catalans in Puerto Rico have underwritten a sum of 19,000 *gourdes* toward an expedition to the east of Saint-Domingue. The expedition is composed of a brig, a schooner and two boats, all of them ill armed, and it brings four hundred men, chosen among all that is most impure on that island. I have been assured that the expedition would begin with the conquest of Samaná. Already this expedition, according to what I have been told, should have departed from Puerto Rico.[29]

Ferrand assured Castel that if the Puerto Ricans showed themselves, they would be received in such a way that they would never return, by the force that Castel had at his disposal and by the crews of the privateer captains Jean Marie, Dumas, and Dominique Yon, who Ferrand supposed were anchored in Samaná. He added:

> If the Puerto Ricans have not yet shown up, whether they are going to attack Samaná or they are going to disembark on the opposite coast, take care to keep your privateers, and soon we will make them repent for having presented themselves before our lands.

The general predicted that the three privateer captains would support Castel, because it would be in their interest to have Samaná kept in French hands.

> Once the Puerto Ricans are repulsed, they will be deported, as well as all the others with similar intents, and we will be at peace.

But Ferrand was not in the situation of sending reinforcements to Castel.

To Face the Invasion from Puerto Rico

On November 1, 1808, Ferrand wrote to Colonel Aussenac, posted in the western part of Santo Domingo, that the Puerto Ricans had come ashore on the eastern coast and that the future of the colony depended on the speed with which they were defeated.[30]

> I depart this morning with four hundred men, and I expect to be back in Santo Domingo in fifteen days.

He warned Aussenac that he could not send him reinforcements, but he gave him a free hand to manage affairs and authorized him to draw funds from the administration. As Aussenac's second in command, he named the commander of the militia of Baní.

While Ferrand marched to the east, Sánchez Ramírez assembled his troops and supplies. In the account that he sent to Montes on November 9, Sánchez Ramírez emphasized the hardships of operating under intense rainfall:

> By dint of working day and night and walking with the last consignment of muskets and munitions, we succeeded in preventing the strike that General Ferrand would surely have in mind. On the 6th of this month I arrived with the last consignment to the Arroyo de Margarito of this jurisdiction of El Seybo where my troops were ill placed and in the open, and with a terrible time of rain, so that all the weapons were wet without means of drying them, on account of the bad weather, which continued.[31]

The Representations of Palo Hincado

According to Gilbert Guillermin, Ferrand left for the east with his troops, but he decided to stop at his hacienda of Higuera-Copal in Samaná, a delay that gave the enemy the opportunity to organize itself.[32] The combat against the rebels and the auxiliary forces that had arrived from Puerto Rico occurred at a place called Palo Hincado. Confident about the superiority of French fighting forces, Ferrand was taken by surprise by the enemy cavalry and by the crossed fire of combatants posted behind trees. Militia from his side defected to the enemy. According to Guillermin, of the five hundred men under Ferrand's command, only forty returned to Santo Domingo.

Sánchez Ramírez' account is more detailed:

> [W]ithout losing time I withdrew with my troops to the place of Palo Hincado (a beautiful location for defense) which I could not accomplish until the morning of the 7th on account of much rain and the flooding of brooks. After I arrived there without stopping a minute, since the messages of my scouts told me that the enemy was coming on us, I arranged the formation of my troops in this way: armed infantry in battle stations on the higher part of the field, a portion of cavalry on the right wing, and another portion on the left, so that the enemy cavalry could not cut us off in any place; between the right wing cavalry and the infantry in a broken terrain in the manner of a ditch that the

height made, I laid an ambush of more than two hundred men with machetes.

Sánchez Ramírez initiated his own legend:

Then, when the enemy was almost in sight, I placed myself in the middle of the field, so that all my army could hear me, and after I had made my exhortation, I shouted in a loud voice: Death to the Leader who calls for retreat, even if it is I myself! Death to the drummer who strikes retreat even if he was ordered to do so! and Death to him who turns his face to the rear, or does not advance at the first charge of musketry without waiting![33]

Sánchez Ramírez also had placed "an ambush of sharpshooters who at the time firing started in the vanguard, would start firing from the enemy's rear." All these dispositions resulted in a rapid denouement. The combat, according to Sánchez Ramírez, did not take "five minutes in putting the Enemy in disorder, without allowing the least military maneuver."[34] On the Dominican side, the losses were six dead and forty-five wounded. The French had three hundred dead and one hundred prisoners. A mounted detachment that pursued the French fugitives found Ferrand's body. He had committed suicide:

[A]shamed of the ugly defeat he had suffered, or exasperated that he could no longer escape from our hands, [he] had taken his own life by a pistol shot. They proved it by bringing me his head, which is well known, the horse he mounted, and the shreds of his uniform.

Sánchez Ramírez availed himself of the victory news by asking Montes for more muskets and help.

Toribio de Montes sent a copy of the report to the Junta, and also his own narrative of the events, in which he naturally highlighted the help he had provided. Nevertheless, some significant details of his narrative were different from that of Sánchez Ramírez. Like the Dominican leader, Montes stated that Ferrand brought a thousand men, which were split between six hundred regular troops and four hundred militia of infantry and cavalry. Montes said that in his disposition at Palo Hincado, Sánchez Ramírez followed the instructions that Montes had sent him. It is interesting that in succeeding communications to the Junta about subsequent events, Montes would reiterate that Sánchez Ramírez knew nothing about military matters but had carefully followed Montes's directives.

On Ferrand's suicide, Montes elaborated:

[D]oubtlessly finding himself exasperated by the ugly defeat he had suffered, lost and in imminent danger of falling in the Spaniards' hands, without being any longer able to escape, he shot himself in the mouth and disfigured half his face on the left side. They cut off his head and that same afternoon presented it held by its whiskers, which were extraordinary, in the general quarter, together with his horse and his insignia.[35]

There is an interesting silence in these initial accounts by Sánchez Ramírez and Montes—neither of them mentioned Tomás Ramírez, the commander of the militia who was with Ferrand, and who changed sides and went over to the insurgents. Did this switch occur during combat or afterward? Did he do it with few or with all his troops?

Tomás Ramírez was mentioned in the account of Palo Hincado that was published in the *Gaceta de Puerto Rico* at the end of November 1808.[36] In general, the account followed the lines of that which Juan Sánchez Ramírez had sent to Toribio de Montes. The anonymous *Gaceta* account stated that "Ferrand had gone out of the city and was very near with regular troops and the national militia of infantry and cavalry commanded by Don Tomás Ramírez." After narrating the words spoken by Sánchez Ramírez and the outcome of the fight, the account proceeded:

The aforementioned Don Tomás Ramírez colonel of the French National Guard has reunited himself with the Spaniards with some men he had under his orders, so that it is thought very few men returned to the City, of more than a thousand who had left it under their General in Chief.[37]

The impression given in this account is that Tomás Ramírez had done his deed after the combat. But the expression that is used, *"se ha reunido a los Españoles,"* does not suggest a surrender, but a change of sides, which obviously would have been more significant before the combat than after it.

In the information that the French general Barquier generated after Ferrand's death and in the account of the battle that Guillermin published in Philadelphia in 1810, Ferrand's defeat is attributed in part to the desertion of the militia at the beginning of the combat.[38] This account suggests that the militia's switch to the other side was a determining factor in Palo Hincado. Much must have weighed in Tomás Ramírez's decision.

But his case was not the only one. If one considers the list of names of the members of the Junta de Bondillo, which met a month after Palo Hincado to ratify Juan Sánchez Ramírez as commanding general, one ascertains that some of those present were former commanders of militia under the French: Diego Polanco, colonel of the dragoon militia of Santiago; Silvestre Aybar, commander of Monte Grande; Diego de Lira, commander of Savana la Mar; and Isidoro de los Santos, commander of Isabela. It was the structure of the Spanish militia itself, preserved by Ferrand, which provided Sánchez Ramírez with an organization for his uprising. The army for the reconquest was not born out of nothing.

British Capture of Samaná

According to Toribio de Montes's account of November 26 to the Supreme Junta in Spain, the British war frigate *Franchise*, which had given escort to the boats carrying military supplies to Sánchez Ramírez at the end of October, then set course toward Samaná. There the British captain, Charles Dashwood, as he had accorded with Montes, took the fort that defended Samaná and captured two French privateers anchored in the port.[39] As per instructions from Sánchez Ramírez, the British captain handed Samaná to Diego de Lira, the commander of the militia of Savana la Mar.

To pay for the boats that had taken the supplies for Sánchez Ramírez, the brig and the schooner returned to Puerto Rico with a cargo of thirty-five fathoms of mahogany,

> which have been sold for the profit of the Royal Treasury in one thousand three hundred and twenty pesos destined for the expenses of these ships, because the Viceroy of Mexico has not sent in more than five years the *situado* for Puerto Rico, so that for 66 months now the garrison has been at half-pay and the employees with innumerable labors, owing those (the Mexican) Royal Funds to this one 3 million pesos.[40]

It is interesting to note how Montes justified the extraction of the valuable Dominican wood. At that time in the Spanish Caribbean, the viceroy of New Spain (i.e., Mexico) stood always at the end of almost every line of exculpation.[41]

In spite of this somber situation, Montes assured the Junta that the boats would return to Santo Domingo with weapons and munitions and two pieces of artillery drawn by horses, "which is proper for war in the mountains," and he offered to send troops and officers to take the capital.[42] And he added:

> As what pertains the former French part which the Blacks possess, they manifest themselves of good faith with the Spaniards, and they have sent a brigadier general offering the needed help, assuring that they have acknowledged Ferdinand VII, and will willingly subject themselves to his obedience, but in spite of that I have warned neither to trust them nor to use of their persons in any way.[43]

It is somewhat difficult to think that Henri Christophe would have proclaimed Ferdinand VII king in the terms in which Montes indicates, or Pétion. What was behind that play of representations—Haitians allegedly supporting Ferdinand VII and Montes saying that the Haitians were disposed to submit themselves to that monarch?

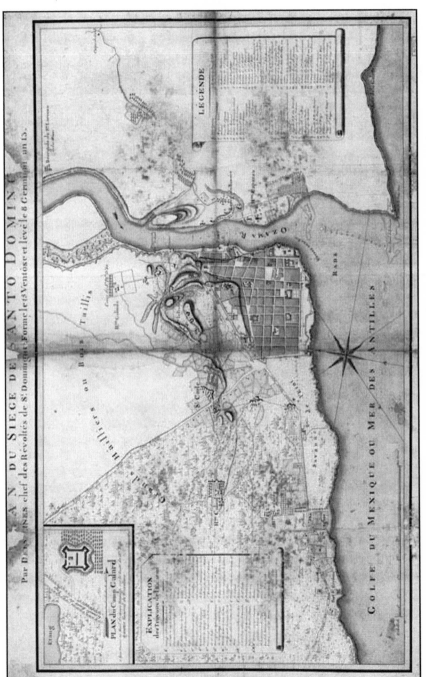

Santo Domingo during the siege.

The Siege and Capitulation of Santo Domingo

Juan Sánchez Ramírez.

Joseph Barquier, Ferrand's second in command, assumed his duties and published a proclamation in which he attempted to project confidence and security. Barquier had a long experience on the island, first in Saint-Domingue under General Leclerc and afterward in Santo Domingo with Ferrand. In 1802, General Leclerc had sent him to Cuba to negotiate in Mexico a loan for his expeditionary force.[1] When Rochambeau, Leclerc's successor, left Saint-Domingue, Barquier was at his side and undertook the tasks that were commended to him.

Barquier's situation after Ferrand's death was extremely difficult. British dominion of the seas denied him real possibilities of effective help either from the metropolis or from Guadeloupe. The loss of Samaná meant not only the disappearance of income from the privateers' prizes but also the possibility of having enough ships to provision the capital.

The Incarceration of Resistors to the French

In spite of Colonel Aussenac's initial success on the western side, the loss of control over the rest of the island was fast. The parish priests fell under the suspicion of promoting adherence to the cause of Ferdinand VII.[2] At least three priests—José Ruiz, Santiago Ruiz, and Vicente Moreno—were jailed for some weeks in Santo Domingo.[3]

The full list of inmates held in jail between September 1808 and June 1809 on the suspicion of disaffection from French rule includes 244 names.[4] The first person detained "as a measure of security," on September 5, 1808, is identified only as "Puerto Rico," but he was released on the following day, on Ferrand's orders. The rhythm of security arrests was uneven (see table 6.1).

TABLE 6.1

Persons Arrested under Security Measures in the Jail of Santo Domingo, September 1808 to June 1809

September 1808 1	February 1809 101
October 1808 4	March 1809 40
November 1808 ... 20	April 1809 16
December 1808 44	May 1809 6
January 1809 8	June 1809 4

Total: 244

Source: Archives Nationales, CC 9 a 45,
"Registre des prisonniers (civil) an XIV-1809."

Some people were arrested twice, in December and in February. Of the 244 arrested, twenty-three died in prison, which is a high rate of mortality. Fourteen of these deaths happened in March and April 1809, when the siege tightened and food became scarce. Perhaps this was the reason so many of the inmates arrested in February were released in March. Eight of the inmates were recruited to serve on the privateer *La Bonne Nouvelle*. About half a dozen escaped either from their labor details or from prison. There were about half a dozen women arrested, apparently servants or attendants of the French, but most of them were promptly released.

The only description provided of the inmates is the race that was ascribed to them and their nationality. In the early period of the security arrests, the Spanish mulattoes prevailed, but after February the white Spaniards arrested were more numerous, as the authorities began to suspect the city's elite, so that even members of officialdom, like Francisco Madrigal and the priest José Ruiz, were arrested. What is interesting is that in the arrests made in May and June, some Frenchmen are listed. The full list of arrests is provided in appendix 1.

Combat Near the Capital

In January 1809, the initial combat in the neighborhood of the capital took place. Barquier tried to prevent the consolidation of the enemies' posts on the other side of the Ozama River, and although he initially had some success in several clashes, as evidenced by his correspondence and by the lists of Dominicans and Puerto Ricans captured in action and later exchanged,[5] he gradually began to lose control of the situation. As Toribio de Montes commented in Puerto Rico, each French casualty diminished Barquier's power because there was no possibility of replacements. In contrast, the forces under Sánchez Ramírez grew from day to day, as reinforcements arrived not only from the island's towns but also from Puerto Rico, from whence several officers of the regular regiment came, as well as a company of artillery and hundreds of volunteers.[6] Also three gunboats arrived.

But the acute problem for Barquier was to supply the capital with provisions. By land, the openings closed one by one. The gunboats sent from Puerto Rico tried to block any effort to bring provisions by sea. In June, the blockade of the port of Santo Domingo was intensified with the additions to the flotilla from Puerto Rico, placed under the command of Ramón Power, who was promoted to warship lieutenant. The final blow was the participation of the British in the siege, not only by sea but also by land.

To surrender to the British or to the forces under Sánchez Ramírez became Barquier's options. On July 6, 1809, under a flag of truce, a French officer approached the British lines with a proposal of capitulation. The British assented to almost all the articles proposed, but they were careful in acknowledging that the forces under Sánchez Ramírez would occupy the city once the French had evacuated. Under the terms of capitulation, the officers would be repatriated to France, but they would not become prisoners of war so long as they agreed not to take up arms against Great Britain and its allies for three years. The soldiers, considered as prisoners of war, would also be returned to France. The whole French garrison would be taken first to Jamaica on British vessels.

While the French garrison left the city, the principal bastions would be occupied, half by the British troops and half by the regular regiment of Puerto Rico. The French could take with them all their archives.

Barquier ratified the capitulation on July 7, 1809, and the process of leaving Santo Domingo began.

Fortunes of the French Military of Santo Domingo

For most of the military, the return to France was not prompt. For the officers, who were eventually taken to the United States, much depended on their ability to book a passage to France. Barquier arrived in France on October 31, 1809, and other members of his staff arrived in either September or October.[7] The squadron chief, Filleul, arrived on February 13, 1810; but Bruce, who had been an aide to Ferrand, was still in the United States in March 1810 and finally returned on April 19 of that year.[8] Around that time arrived some sergeants and corporals who had received provisional promotions to officers in Santo Domingo.

Of the soldiers, the trace is lost more easily. During the Napoleonic Wars, captured French soldiers were sometimes exchanged for British prisoners in French hands, but other times they spent years as captives on ships anchored in British ports.

Some members of the French forces chose to stay in Santo Domingo, either because they had married there or because they represented no major problem to the new authorities. Among them there were some Italians.

Sánchez Ramírez' Way

In a congress of delegates from the townships celebrated at Bondillo on December 12, 1808, Ferdinand VII was recognized as king of Spain, and the Supreme Central Junta of Madrid (relocated from Seville) as the representative of his authority. The delegates added:

> In attention to the merit which he has acquired being the Caudillo and motor of the glorious enterprise of the People of Santo Domingo rising from the shameful yoke of the tyrant Napoleon Emperor of the French, and in view of the protection which by his means he has merited from Don Toribio de Montes Field Marshall of the Royal Armies, Governor, Intendant and Captain General of the Island of Puerto Rico, the junta names as provisional political and military governor and intendant Don Juan Sánchez Ramírez commanding general of the Spanish Army of Santo Domingo until Her Highness the Supreme Central Junta of Madrid provides.[9]

The third article of their agreements sought to define the future relations between Sánchez Ramírez and the Junta that had elected him:

> The Governor from now on will convoke the members of the Junta whenever he wishes, and he will be its president, in the intelligence that it only retains a consultative voice and the decision belongs only to the Governor.

Therefore there was no break with the traditional system of government, since the Junta could only be convoked at the Governor's wish and would only proffer opinions, but the final determination of matters would be in the hands of Sánchez Ramírez. But the mere fact that the Junta became institutionalized bears interest.

By its fourth article of the Junta's agreements, "the administrative system and the judicial order will remain as before until the City of Santo Domingo is taken, when there will be a provisional organization according to the Laws of the Kingdom, and municipal ordinances." Finally it was agreed that Sánchez Ramírez would swear an oath of fidelity to the king and of obedience to Spanish laws. They agreed to send an original copy in duplicate to the Supreme Junta and a copy to the governor of Puerto Rico, "whom the Junta recognizes as Protector of the enterprise," and also copies to the cities, towns, and inhabited places of the Spanish part of the island.

Some people have asked about the representative character of this junta, which as any revolutionary organism claimed general support without necessarily possessing the credentials to make it evident. The same could be asked about other contemporary juntas, both in Spain and in America. In any case, in Santo Domingo, the priority was to expel the French from the capital, and while that joint effort gathered all the energies, there seems not to have been substantial open questioning of the agreements taken at Bondillo.

The Summer of 1809: No Help Forthcoming

Once the euphoria over the taking of the capital passed, Juan Sánchez Ramírez faced the bitter reality that there were no funds to maintain a permanent army, and much less to make improvements and repairs to the defenses of the city. It is true that there was no imminent danger of the return of the French, but there was the disquieting proximity of the Haitians and also the possibility of a coup by some faction who wanted to seize power.

The request he placed with Salvador Meléndez, the new governor of Puerto Rico, had a discouraging answer. Meléndez answered:

> Do you think that at the end of so many years in which we have not received funds to replace the consumption of the royal

warehouses, there are going to be bullets, bombs, grenades, gunpowder, lead, rigging, rum, and items for artillery and sappers, and I am not saying surplus from our garrison to give, since we have never had the full complement, but not even enough to live with a steady confidence? I have just asked Mexico for gunpowder and armaments. The warehouse items are not provided nor produced by the island itself.[10]

Meléndez emphasized that his principal responsibility was the security of his stronghold and of the entire island. "I am accountable to the King, if I do not gather all the forces with which my fate has endowed me to discharge my part." He urged Sánchez Ramírez to appeal to the Spanish Junta "to organize, provide, endow and expedite whatever is necessary for the defense and the conservation of the conquest." He was sarcastic about the fate of the battalion of Santo Domingo, which apparently Sánchez Ramírez was asking to be returned to his capital:

Do you think that the battalion of Santo Domingo came here? They have deceived you. The battalion was sacrificed on the plains of [Port au] Prince by Toussaint. Here those who could escape arrived, and afterward the standards, the empty funds, and the archive saved by its leader. Almost the same can be said about the artillerymen, except those whom Toussaint ordered to be slaughtered or shot, but of those I am sending you seventeen men, that with seven who are there and one who is sick and will go later make twenty-three artillerymen, who are those I can spare, while all the others who have gone there to help, to the total of twenty-eight, should come back.

Meléndez was profuse in his praise of Sánchez Ramírez, but the artillerymen noted above were all that he yielded. Sánchez Ramírez also wrote to Juan Villavicencio, commanding general of Havana's shipyard:

Having taken this city, and our enemy having consumed or exported whatever was useful in it, the needs have considerably risen and not the resources. Trade, like a child whom it is necessary to caress to attract him, cannot actually suffer high taxes or exactions. Agriculture needs to liven up because having been almost a year without the men who constitute its principal strength, it is languid and dejected. The well-to-do have suffered losses and expenses that absolutely hinder them from taking loans without donations which are insufficient.[11]

Sánchez Ramírez also explained that it was no solution to sell the confiscated properties to the French, since there were no buyers and one would have to market them too cheaply. As for the troops, both the patriots and the auxiliaries from Puerto Rico had received no compensation, because they did not even receive a reward "as it is accustomed when a city is taken." He added:

> With the campaign, so to speak, ended, having achieved the enterprise, the enthusiasm ceased that moved the desire, and that served as pay, reward and everything, and meanwhile everything is in need of repairs—the walls, the artillery, public buildings, streets, offices.

To solve these matters external help was necessary:

> From Puerto Rico I have reason to believe that nothing will be sent me outside of miserable resources, and those with eternal delays.

He has decided to send to the viceroy of New Spain Don José Melgares, "an officer which Your Excellency [Villavicencio] has wished to put under my orders . . . on the packet-boat *Coira*, which had been taken as a prize by the ships that blocked the city, I have taken for the King." The hope was that the viceroy would send the requested sums. Sánchez Ramírez asked Villavicencio for his intercession with the viceroy and observed:

> The depopulation that this island has suffered on account of the different vicissitudes it has undergone, make me wish for the return of the emigrant families spread throughout His Majesty's dominions in this America. . . . [H]aving been in a state of war and it being impossible to keep up such an armed force as is necessary to make this colony respectable, it requires a number of men enlisted in the militia who may take up arms in a necessary event, and supply for the lack of the indicated troops.

The communication to the viceroy, dated August 18, 1809, was no less urgent. After repeating some of the observations made to Villavicencio, Sánchez Ramírez specified:

The goods taken from the French as legitimate prizes are our only resource, but the outcome was slow, because the lumber, cattle and other articles that compose them would have to be liquidated at a vile price in order to reduce it to coin with the promptitude that the execution of the urgencies requires.[12]

Apparently the efforts were unsuccessful, because on November 17, 1809, Sánchez Ramírez again addressed the viceroy to ask for military supplies:

[B]ecause the government of Puerto Rico to whom lately I had recourse in request of those supplies, and in the same way about the troop that garrisoned this place, has answered me with an absolute negative, of which I also include a copy to Your Excellency in proof that there remains for me no other hope in the urgent state of this fortress, that the help from the capital of New Spain . . . since from Spain it would be temerity to hope anything of this when all possible contributions must be sent there.[13]

He took the occasion to provide an account of past assistance:

[I]n the last war with the French, a time when the Spanish part of this island was in its whole given, helped by troops from Spain, Puerto Rico, Caracas and Havana, the Kingdom of Mexico also helped with a regiment, whose actual state and the lack of help from other parts, has come to be quite reduced, and the least one can request in terms of troops to garrison and make this fortress and island secure, in whose reconquest the enemies of Spain and of the whole human race, the perverse followers of Napoleon, will place all their effort they can in the present circumstances.

The French menace still seemed credible. José Melgares returned from his mission to Mexico in February 1810, but without the one hundred thousand pesos that the Viceroy had destined for Santo

Domingo, "but instead with sixty-nine thousand and a bit on account of the discount that the Marine at Havana made on account of the help it had contributed at the beginning of the reconquest."[14] In May 1810, the intendant of Havana sent ten thousand pesos, "by way of Puerto Rico," but the governor of Puerto Rico intercepted them "in part of payment for the help given."[15] Consequently, in July Sánchez Ramírez again appealed to the viceroy, explaining that "[as] the needs increase[,] resources become scarce in a totally ruined country, which demands large income to begin to recover although with a slowness of its incalculable past disgraces."

He deplored the rebellion in Caracas, because it had deprived Santo Domingo of help decreed by the Spanish Junta:

> The criminal scandalous rebellion in the province of Caracas is another blow that has been deeply felt in the matter of help because His Majesty having resolved by royal order in January that the same *situado* for here amount to three hundred thousand pesos and a bit more, and that half of that sum come from those funds, which were nearby, I tried to equip a ship of war to obtain with promptitude such considerable help without being in the straits of having frequent recourse to that kingdom [i.e., Mexico], but at the time of departure there arrived the detailed news of the novelty of their strange revolution, and it was necessary to suspend it and worry myself in search of at least the means to maintain the troops until I found the occasion to present it to Your Excellency, who is my only hope, as I do now, beseeching you, in the name of the King we worship in common, that in spite of the penury of those funds, you please move the last efforts to send me at the greatest brevity an amount.[16]

On September 16, 1810, shortly after this letter was sent, Miguel Hidalgo made his appeal for the revolution for Mexican independence. Sánchez Ramírez died in February 1811,[17] and an interim governor took the helm until the Junta in Spain named a successor.

Haitian Attitudes

From the beginning, Toribio de Montes had been the one who had been most attentive to Haiti. First he repeatedly warned Sánchez Ramírez not to ask for or accept help from Henri Christophe, who governed the northern part of Haiti. But Montes's attitude toward Haiti changed in 1809. Since help from the other Spanish dominions was not forthcoming, and beyond the twenty thousand pesos that Villavicencio had initially sent to Sánchez Ramírez, neither Cuba nor Caracas sent money, Toribio de Montes wrote directly to Christophe and to Pétion, asking for supplies for Sánchez Ramírez's troops. Christophe answered immediately, sending a subordinate to Puerto Rico with a cargo of muskets and supplies for the Dominicans. Pétion also answered with direct help to Sánchez Ramírez. Originally feared as threats, the Haitians had become allies.

Internal Opposition: Ciriaco Ramírez

For reasons that have not become clear, Ciriaco Ramírez did not participate in the Junta de Bondillo of December 1808. Possibly the explanation is that Colonel Aussenac, who commanded the French in battle on the western front, had not yet been defeated and was active in the sector where Ciriaco Ramírez supposedly was coordinating the war.

In 1811, charges of insubordination were formulated against Ciriaco Ramírez and he was sent to Puerto Rico.

The Return of the Emigrants

On January 5, 1810, the Supreme Junta in Spain decreed

> that in the precise term of four months after the publication of this order, all the families and persons who migrated from the island on account of its cession to France be restored to the island of Santo Domingo, for which purpose transportation on

the Royal Treasury's account will be provided and their pensions will be paid for a year after their arrival at Santo Domingo so that it may serve as a help in their settlement.[18]

If the emigrants did not return, the Junta added, they would only keep their pensions for the four months appointed for their return to the island. It is hard to determine how many obeyed the Junta's decree. In some cases, it is possible that some member of the emigrant family had returned to claim the properties and evaluate the propitious moment for the return of the rest of the family. There is a draft of a letter by the governor of Puerto Rico to the governor of Santo Domingo asking for his good offices in getting the notary Angel M. Novoa to return to the town of Aguada, where he was the public's and the *cabildo*'s notary. He had been given a four-month leave of absence to return to Santo Domingo, but he had overextended his leave. Apparently the same letter was written concerning Eloy Tirado, the notary at San Germán.[19] But there is little evidence of a massive return of the emigrants, especially of those who had left in the first years after the transfer of command.

Conclusion

British ships in the harbor at Kingston, Jamaica, 1870s.

The figure of Marie-Louis Ferrand has remained opaque in the historical memory. One looks in vain for him in Napoleon's correspondence. Guillermin, the first chronicler of his downfall, portrayed him as a person "affable by education and violent in character."[1] Later French historians hardly stayed to consider him. In general, disinterest in the affairs of Saint-Domingue and Santo Domingo began with the death of General Leclerc, Napoleon's brother-in-law.

Neither has Dominican historiography been generous with Ferrand. His successes in the five years in which he was Captain General are summarily dismissed, and the interest is dedicated rather to his defeat at Palo Hincado. It is as if Ferrand's administration was an interruption in an already traced history. National histories tend to be that way, to discard everything that does not contribute to the elaboration of a coherent and unidirectional national past.

But what if we assume a broader perspective and attempt to situate the French administration of Santo Domingo within a panoramic vision of the Caribbean? What if we see Santo Domingo as the laboratory where the transplanting of French institutions that promoted rationalization, secularization, and modernization was rehearsed? May we not examine matters other than those belonging to the established and inherited national discourse? May we not represent the failure of the French project in Santo Domingo as a signal of the general resistance in the Spanish Caribbean to the French revolutionary program? Would not the slowness with which the Spanish Caribbean adopted the abolition of the slave trade and slavery itself, the Creole reluctance to extend schooling to all children, and the enormous silence in writing about equal rights and equal opportunities in a republic where all citizens would be equal before the law all constitute evidence of that resistance?

Could we not contrast the effect that the British occupation of Havana in the 1760s had on the development of Cuba to the arrested development of Santo Domingo after 1808?

Consequences of the Displacement of the French from Santo Domingo

The French Revolution and the Haitian Revolution made the French-speaking Caribbean the focus of interest in the Caribbean at the end of the eighteenth and the beginning of the nineteenth century. The departure of the French from Santo Domingo in 1808 marks one of the important stages at the end of that leading role. At the moment, it was not that evident. Until the end of Napoleon's regime and even at the beginning of the reign of Louis XVIII, there were proposals, plans, and schemes to reconquer Saint-Domingue.[2] In many of those projects, the enterprise would begin with the occupation of Samaná or one of the ports in the Spanish part of the island. A good example of these plans is the one drawn by Ferrand's former aide, Castel-La Boulbène, now a lieutenant colonel. Received at the Ministry of

Marine and Colonies in June 1814, the proposal is redolent of optimism:

> Preliminary dispositions. First: occupy the Spanish part of the island until there is a perfect and peaceful possession of the French part, because it is important for the army and the security of operations to have behind it a fortress [Santo Domingo] that may guarantee its food supplies and its hospitals, and a vast port [Samaná] that will make the fleet safe.[3]

The illusion of many French emigrants, settled in Louisiana, Cuba, Puerto Rico, and France itself, was to return to the island. But the operation began taking on airs of unreality. The abolition of the international slave trade, to which France finally adhered, eliminated the possibility of recolonizing the island with slave labor. The costs of such an expedition began to look unmanageable. Again, there was no question that the British would be inclined to cooperate, since the revitalization of agriculture in Saint-Domingue would confer on them no benefit but would help lower British sugar prices.[4] Also the French crown, attentive to the dismantling of the Spanish Empire in America, came to entertain other possibilities, such as the purchase or the acquisition by other means of Cuba or Puerto Rico. Finally the treaty between the government of Charles X and the Haitian president Boyer and the subsequent project of Algeria erased from the map the illusion of Saint-Domingue.[5]

For Haiti the erasure of French power from Santo Domingo removed the nightmare of having the French as neighbors. While Christophe cherished the relationship with Great Britain, Boyer sought a diplomatic solution with France. In both cases, the aim was to exorcise the specter of a new French armed intervention.

Was French power in the Caribbean definitely overshadowed? As late as 1825, a visit to the western Caribbean by a French naval squadron worried authorities in the United Sates sufficiently for Secretary of State Henry Clay to write to James Brown, an American minister in France, to convey the American wish that in the future such visits would be informed beforehand to the American authorities and to remind the French government that the United States could not look with indifference that the islands of Cuba and Puerto Rico pass from the power of Spain to that of any other European power.[6] But after 1825, whatever might happen in Europe, France was no longer an element of weight in Caribbean geopolitics.

The Uncertain Future of Santo Domingo

As for Santo Domingo, the disenchantment experienced after the triumphal entry of the revolutionaries in the capital in 1809 never dissipated. The rest of the Spanish Empire in America had then its own agendas, and it was not inclined to help the Dominicans decisively. The feat that had been achieved would be insufficiently valued by others.

The period that the Dominican historians have called La España Boba ("lethargic Spain"), between 1809 and 1822, marked the virtual abandonment of Santo Domingo by the metropolis. When the Mexican *situado* to other colonies was definitely abolished in 1821, the metropolitan government instructed the viceroy of New Spain

> that in the future . . . not only Havana, but also the Philippine Islands, Puerto Rico and the province of Yucatán fit their expenditures to their own revenues and resources, to subsist with the same without counting on any other help but their own funds, leaving nevertheless to the care and zeal of Your Excellency to help, as you offer, the island of Santo Domingo so long as it needs it.[7]

This exception was of little use to Santo Domingo since, in that same year, Mexico achieved its independence from Spain and its obligations to other Spanish colonies ceased.

After Christophe died and Pétion's successor in the south, Jean-Pierre Boyer, reunited both halves of Haiti, Haiti was more openly perceived as a menace. In January 1821, the Spanish government wrote to the captain general of Cuba asking him to send resources and supplies to Cuba. The governor of Santo Domingo wrote on April 23, 1821, to his peer in Puerto Rico, citing the order send to Cuba and asking for help:

All the Spanish provinces that have slavery should interest themselves in the defense, security and conservation of the Spanish part of the island, because if those people come to appropriate themselves of it, they will place themselves in immediate contact with the other islands, both Spanish and foreign, and in all of them slaves will rise with ease, or they [the Haitians] will provide the most secure asylum to an emigration that can hardly be contained, and much less from that island [Puerto Rico] that already has had so many experiences of it. . . . Consider what will happen when far from being someone to apprehend and deliver the fugitives, there be someone who calls them, opens the door to them and receives them with open arms.[8]

The governor of Puerto Rico answered that there were no resources available on the island, but offered sympathy: "I will make as many efforts as I can so that Your Excellency may repel the aggressions of those neighbors."[9]

Lacking outside help, Dominicans found it necessary to devise their own solutions. Sánchez Ramírez's successor as captain general encouraged landholders to plant what they were going to consume, but that only won him the nickname Carlos Conuco. In spite of the advantages that a planting program of subsistence crops offered to a zone vulnerable to disasters, there was no will to become a peasant society.

Another solution was the proclamation of independence, which was being tried out in other parts of the Spanish Empire. The so-called Conspiracy of the Italians, an allusion to the febrile plans of some foreigners remaining from Ferrand's time in Santo Domingo, had its parallels in other parts; even in Florida there was then a pro-independence conspiracy.[10] That conspiracy failed because at the moment it did not reflect an aspiration of the Creoles who had risen against Ferrand and could do so again.

Then came the short-lived independence proclaimed by Nuñez Cáceres.[11] That it was not the opportune moment was shown by the ease with which Boyer's Haitian troops assumed power. This act provoked a new emigration of Dominicans to Cuba and Puerto Rico. Even Silvestre Aybar, who had been commander of Monte Grande under Ferrand and was a member of the Junta de Bondillo in December 1808, moved to Puerto Rico, where in 1825 he became *teniente a guerra* (the equivalent to the municipal authority) in Utuado.[12]

Reconfiguration of the Relationship between Spain and Great Britain

The disappearance of France as an immediate neighbor of the Spanish colonies and the intervention of Great Britain in the expulsion of the French entailed a new relationship between Spain and Britain. Allies in the Peninsular War against Napoleon, they were uncomfortably positioned at the time of the wars of independence in Spanish America. It was in Great Britain that the rebels obtained financing, while muskets of British origin acquired in Saint Thomas harassed the Spanish troops on the continent, and there were thousands of British veterans from the Napoleonic Wars that supported the insurgents. But Spain could neither invoke French help against Great Britain, as in the old days of the Bourbon alliance, nor was it possible to challenge the most powerful state that emerged from the Congress of Vienna.

The United States as a Balance to British Naval Power

The diminished role of the French in the Caribbean Sea after their expulsion from Santo Domingo left the British as lords of Caribbean waters. It is true that in the War of 1812 against United States, they had to face North American privateers in those waters, but the operations of these privateers did little to sever communications among the British islands and between these and the metropolis. Although a French squadron made some display of its flag around the waters of Cuba after 1820, nobody expected a return to the old Anglo-French rivalry.

It was the United States that increased its naval presence in the Caribbean, first with the purpose of liberating its own trade from the pirates and privateers which in the beginning of the 1820s plagued the sea lanes between the islands. Then other interests began to complement those efforts, and although the Monroe Doctrine was at that time backed with limited navy strength, the very affirmation of a policy of maintaining the European powers at a distance from the possibility of empire in the lands of the decaying Spanish Empire justified the repeated patrols and naval actions of its squadrons in Caribbean waters.

APPENDIX 1

Arrests of Persons Jailed in Santo Domingo on Suspicion of Possible Subversion, September 1808 to June 1809

1. "Puerto Rico." Spanish mulatto. Jailed September 5, 1808, as a measure of security. Released September 6, 1808, by order of the general in chief.

2. Ambrosio Soler. White Spaniard. October 5, 1808. Arrested by the commissioner of police as a dangerous man, having had seditious purposes. This man had been deported from the colony for bad conduct and he has reentered without authorization. No release date.

3. Mateo de Dios. Spanish mulatto. October 8, 1808. For suspicion and as a measure of security. Released April 14, 1809, by order of the commander of the army.

4. Lacroze. White Frenchman. October 14, 1808. As a security measure. Released March 8, 1809, by order of the general in chief.

5. Walton. American white. October 26, 1808. As a security measure. Released February 13, 1809, by order of the general in chief.

6. José Lorenzo Méndez. Spanish mulatto. November 1, 1898. For security measures. Died in prison April 17, 1809.

7. Pasqual. French black man. November 1, 1808. As a security measure. Released November 23, 1808, to join the colonial legion, by order of the Commander of the army.

8. Juan de Azevedo. White Spaniard. November 7, 1808. Arrested by the commissioner of police for having had resolves against the

Source: CC 9 a 45, "Registre des prisonniers (civil) an XIV-1809" (name, description, date of arrest, charge, date of release or death).

105

government. Released December 1, 1808, by order of the commander of the army.

9. Juan Maldonado. White Spaniard. November 9, 1808. Arrested by the commissioner of police as a measure of security. Released February 13, 1809, by order of the general in chief.

10. Ambrosio Eusebio. Black Spaniard. November 9, 1808. As a measure of security. Died in prison February 17, 1809.

11. Manuel de los Reyes. Spanish mulatto. November 10, 1808. For suspicion and as a measure of security. Released March 18, 1809, by order of the commander of the army.

12. Francisco Bertrand. Spanish mulatto. November 11, 1808. For vagrancy and as a measure of security. Released December 11, 1808, by order of the commander of the army.

13. Joseph Saintes. Black Frenchman. November 12, 1808. For vagrancy and as measure of security. Died in prison January 29, 1809.

14. Manuel Fina. Spanish mulatto. November 14, 1808. As a measure of security. Released December 13, 1808, by order of the commander of the army.

15. Thomas Morcelo. Black Spaniard. November 16, 1808. As a measure of security. Released November 25, 1808, by order of the commander of the army.

16. Dargegnan. Black Frenchman. November 18, 1808. As a measure of security. Released January 29, 189, by order of the commander of the army.

17. José Gausot. Black Frenchman. November 18, 1808. As a measure of security. Released November 22, 1808, by order of the commander of the army.

18 and 19. Jean and Denis Durand. Black Frenchmen. As a measure of security. Released February 13, 1809, by order of the general in chief.

20. José Fernández. Black Spaniard. November 23, 1808. Arrested by the commissioner of police as a measure of security. Released November 23, 1808, by order of the commander of the army.

21. Manuel Cavero. White Spaniard. November 23, 1808. As a measure of security. Released April 27, 1809, by order of the general in chief, he was put aboard the *Beau Narcisse.*

22. Merlin. White Frenchman. November 29, 1808. As a measure of security. Died in prison on March 9, 1809.

23. Phelipe Santiago. He belongs to Ruiz's father. November 29, 1808. For sanctions and as a security measure. Released December 25, 1808, by order of the general in chief.

24. María Encarnación. Black Spanish woman. November 30, 1808. For suspicion and as a measure of security. No Released date given.

25. Juan. Black Spanish. November 30, 1808. For suspicion and as a measure of security. Released February 10, 1809, by order of the commander of the army.

26. José de Mendoza. White Spaniard. Musician attached to the Fifth Regiment. December 6, 1808. Jailed as a dangerous man and very bad subject. Died in prison on May 5, 1809.

27. Lanny Soulmon. White Frenchman. December 7, 1808. As a measure of security. Released January 23, 1809, by order of the general in chief.

28. Joseph Bernard. Dutch mulatto. December 10, 1808. As a measure of security. Released December 26, 1808, by order of the commander of the army.

29. Chavarie. White Spaniard. December 14, 1808. As a measure of security. Released February 13, 1809, by order of the general in chief.

30. Diego Ascaño. White Spaniard. December 14, 1808. As a measure of security. Released January 31, 1809, by order of the general in chief.

31. Martines id. [*sic*] White Spaniard. December 14, 1808. As a measure of security. Released January 21, 1809 by order of the general in chief.

32. Gregorio García. White Spaniard. December 14, 1808. As a measure of security. Released February 13, 1809, by order of the general in chief.

33. Felis de la Peña. White Spaniard. December 14, 1808. As a measure of security. Released February 13, 1809, by order of the general in chief.

34. Joaquin Gatel. White Spaniard. December 14, 1808. As a measure of security. Released February 13, 1809, by order of the general in chief.

35. Antonio Morales. White Spaniard. December 14, 1808. As a measure of security. Released February 13, 1809, by order of the general in chief.

36. José Ruiz. White Spaniard. December 14, 1808. As a measure of security. Released February 13, 1809, by order of the general in chief.

37. Vicente Moreno. White Spaniard. December 14, 1808. As a measure of security. Released February 13, 1809, by order of the general in chief.

38. Santiago Ruiz. White Spaniard. December 14, 1808. As a measure of security. Released February 13, 1809, by order of the general in chief.

39. Francisco Madrigal. White Spaniard. December 14, 1808. As a measure of security. Released February 13, 1809, by order of the general in chief.

40. Cayetano Garry. White Spaniard. December 14, 1808. As a measure of security. Released February 13, 1809, by order of the general in chief.

41. Salvador Martínez. White Spaniard. December 14, 1808. As a measure of security. Released February 13, 1809, by order of the general in chief.

42. Francisco Robayna. White Spaniard. December 15, 1808. As a measure of security. Released February 13, 1809, by order of the general in chief.

43. Marcel Valderon. Spanish mulatto. December 15, 1808. As a measure of security. Released February 13, 1809, by order of the general in chief.

44. Santos Peña. Spanish mulatto. December 15, 1808. As a measure of security. He left on April 13, 1809, by order of the general in chief.

45. Robles. Spanish mulatto. December 15, 1808. As a measure of security. He left on April 13, 1809, by order of the general in chief.

46. José Torres. Spanish mulatto. December 15, 1808. As a measure of security. Released April 13, 1809, by order of the general in chief.

47. Gregorio Ladina. Spanish mulatto. December 15, 1808. As a measure of security. Released April 13, 1809, by order of the general in chief.

48. Miguel Perdomo. White Spaniard. December 15, 1808. As a measure of security. Released April 13, 1809, by order of the general in chief.

49. Gravié Mella. White Spaniard. December 15, 1808. As a measure of security. Released April 13, 1809, by order of the general in chief.

50. Féliz. White Spaniard. December 15, 1808. As a measure of security. Released April 13, 1809, by order of the general in chief.

51. Mathias Roz. White Spaniard. December 15, 1808. As a measure of security. Released December 17, 1808, by order of the general in chief.

52. Aba. White Spaniard. December 15, 1808. As a measure of security. Released February 13, 1809, by order of the general in chief.

53. Razon. White Spaniard. December 15, 1808. As a measure of security. February 13, 1809, by order of the general in chief.

54. Jean Jacques. Black Frenchman, belonging to M. Muler. December 15, 1808. As a measure of security. December 16, 1808, on the request of M. Bailly, by order of the commander of the army,

55. Juan de la Cruz. Black Spaniard, belonging to Antonio Ramírez. December 15, 1808. As a measure of security. Released March 31, 1809, by order of the commander of the army.

56. Juan Luciano. Free French mulatto. December 15, 1808. As a measure of security. Died in prison on March 8, 1809.

57. Francisco Rodríguez. White Spaniard. December 16, 1808. As measure of security. He left January 7, 1809, by order of the general in chief.

58. Manuel Acoste, it is said that his name is Andrés Cuña. Spanish mulatto. December 16, 1808. As a measure of security. Died in prison on March 30, 1809.

59. Bonetty. White Italian. December 17, 1808. For suspicion and as a measure of security. Released January 18, 1809, by order of the commander of the army.

60. Brandy. White Italian. December 18, 1808. Arrested by the commissary of police as a measure of security. Released February 11, 1809, by order of the commander of the army.

61. Louis Flaure. Black Spaniard. December 18, 1808. Arrested by the

commissary of police as a measure of security. Died in prison on April 27, 1809.

62. Jacques Mondion. French mulatto. Rifleman of the colonial legion. December 19, 1808. As a measure of security. Released December 27, 1808, by order of the commander of the army.

63. Joseph Robert. Spanish mulatto. Rifleman of the colonial legion. December 19, 1808. As a measure of security. Released April 13, 1809, to board *La Sentinelle* by order of the general in chief.

64. Miguel Loriano. White Spaniard. December 20, 1808. Arrested by the commissary of police as a measure of security. Released February 13, 1809, by order of the commander of the army.

65. Pedro Bertrand. Black Spaniard. December 20, 1808. Arrested by the commissary of police as a measure of security. On April 6, 1809, he escaped from the government's public works.

66. Juan Azevedo. White Spaniard. December 26, 1808. Arrested by the commissary of police as a measure of security. Released February 4, 1809, by order of the commander of the army,

67. Santiago Bello. Spanish mulatto. December 30, 1808. Arrested by the commissary of Police as a measure of security. Died in prison January 6, 1809.

68. Miguel Pastor. Spanish mulatto. December 30, 1808. Arrested by the commissary of police as a measure of security. Released January 4, 1809, by order of the commander of the army.

69. Phelipe Santiago. Black Spaniard, belonging to Father Ruiz. December 31, 1808. As a measure of security. Died in prison January 27, 1809.

70. José Ximenes. Black Spaniard, belonging to Father Moreno. He says his name is José Vinomercano. January 3, 1809. As a measure of security. Released March 20, 1809, by order of the commander of the army.

71. Janvier. Black Frenchman. January 4, 1809. Released February 7, 1809, by order of the commander of the army.

72. María Antonia. Black Spanish woman. January 6, 1809. As a measure of security. Released February 6, 1809, by order of the commander of the army.

73. Phelipe. Black Spaniard. January 6, 1809. As a measure of security. Released January 8, 1809, by order of the commander of the army.

74. Manuel Severino. Black Spaniard. January 16, 1809. For suspicion and as a measure of security. Released March 17, 1809, by order of the commander of the army.

75. Domingo de Soza. Spanish mulatto. March 23, 1809. As a security measure. Released February 13, 1809, by order of the commander of the army.

76. José Pereyra. Spanish mulatto. January 23, 1809. As a measure of security. Released February 13, 1809, by order of the commander of the army.

77. Benito de Soto. Black Spaniard. January 31, 1809. Arrested by the commissioner of police for suspicion and for murder. Died in prison April 28, 1809.

78. Diego Soler. [No description.] October 15, 1808, for suspicion. Released March 18, 1809, by order of the commander of the army.

79. Antonio Figueroa. Black Spaniard. A slave of a Spanish insurgent. February 6, 1809. Arrested by a citizen while plundering. Died in prison March 14, 1809.

80. Manuel de Jesús. Spanish mulatto. February 14, 1809. As a measure of security. Released March 18, 1809, by order of the commander of the army.

81. Antoine. Black Frenchman, belonging to M. Soucher. February 15, 1809. As a measure of security. Released February 26, 1809, by order of the commander of the army.

82. José Ruiz (priest). White Spaniard. February 19, 1809. As a measure of security. Released March 10, 1809, by order of the general in chief.

83. Santiago Ruiz (priest). White Spaniard. February 19, 1809. As a measure of security. Released March 12, 1809, by order of the general in chief.

84. Vicente Moreno (priest). White Spaniard. February 19, 1809. As a measure of security. Released March 18, 1809, by order of the general in chief.

85. Francisco Madrigal. White Spaniard. February 19, 1809. As a measure of security. Released March 18, 1809, by order of the general in chief.

86. Gregorio García. White Spaniard. February 19, 1809. As a measure of security. Released on March 15, 1809, by order of the general in chief.

87. Joaquín Gatel. White Spaniard. February 19, 1809. As a measure of security. Released March 10, 1809, by order of the general in chief.

88. Manuel Perdomo. White Spaniard. February 19, 1809. As a measure of security. Released March 18, 1809, by order of the general in chief.

89. Cayetano García. White Spaniard. February 19, 1809. As a measure of security. Released March 18, 1809, by orders of the general in chief.

90. Ramón Martínez. White Spaniard. February 19, 1809. As a measure of security. Released March 15, 1809.

91. Abad. White Spaniard. February 19, 1809. As a measure of security. Released March 18, 1809.

92. Gregorio Ladina. White Spaniard. February 19, 1809. As a measure of security. Released March 17, 1809, by order of the general in chief.

93. Salvador Martinez. White Spaniard. February 19, 1809. As a measure of security. Released March 17, 1809, by order of the general in chief.

94. Domingo de Soza. White Spaniard. February 19, 1809. As a measure of security. Released March 12, 1809, by order of the general in chief.

95. Gravier Mella. White Spaniard. February 19, 1809. As a measure of security. Released March 15, 1809 by order of the General in Chief.

96. Juan de Dios de Muesas. White Spaniard. February 19, 1809. As a measure of security. Released March 17, 1809, by order of the general in chief.

97. Mathias Ruiz. White Spaniard. February 19, 1809. As a measure of security. Released March 4, 1809, by order of the general in chief.

98. Fernando Aponte. White Spaniard. February 19, 1809. As a measure of security. Released March 17, 1809, by order of the general in chief.

99. José Martínez. White Spaniard. February 19, 1809. As a measure of security. Released March 15, 1809, by order of the general in chief.

100. Antonio González. White Spaniard. February 19, 1809. As a measure of security. Released March 17, 1809, by order of the general in chief.

101. Diego Ascanio. White Spaniard. February 19, 1809. As a measure of security. Released March 12, 1809, by order of the general in chief.

102. Martines Ascanio. White Spaniard. February 19, 1809. As a measure of security. Released March 12, 1809, by order of the general in chief.

103. Feliz Soler. White Spaniard. February 19, 1809. As a measure of security. Released February 28, 1809, by order of the general in chief.

104. Llavaria. White Spaniard. February 19, 1809. As a measure of security. Released February 28, 1809, by order of the general in chief.

105. José Sánchez. White Spaniard. February 19, 1809. As a measure of security. Released March 16, 1809, by order of the general in chief.

106. José Ponse. White Spaniard. February 19, 1809. As a measure of security. Released March 17, 1809, by order of the general in chief.

107. Juan de Azevedo. White Spaniard. February 19, 1809. As a measure of security. Released March 25, 1809, by order of the general in chief.

108. Miguel Acostas. White Spaniard. February 19, 1809. As a measure of security. Released March 14, 1809, by order of the general in chief.

109. Juan Antonio Durand. White Spaniard. February 19, 1809. As a measure of security. Released March 25, 1809, by order of the general in chief.

110. José Pereyra. Spanish mulatto. February 19, 1809. As a measure of security. Released March 18, 1809, by orders of the general in chief.

111. Feliz de la Peña. Spanish mulatto. February 19, 1809. As a measure of security. Released March 18, 1809, by orders of the general in chief.

112. Francisco Urbano. Spanish mulatto. February 19, 1809. As a measure of security. Released March 16, 1809, by orders of the general in chief.

113. Francisco Rodríguez. Spanish mulatto. February 19, 1809. As a measure of security. Released March 17, 1809, by order of the general in chief.

114. Alexandro Fernández. Spanish mulatto. February 19, 1809. As a measure of security. Released March 16, 1809, by order of the general in chief.

115. Ramon Jepes. Spanish mulatto. February 19, 1809. As a measure of security. Released March 16, 1809, by order of the general in chief.

116. Francisco Robayna. Spanish mulatto. February 19, 1809. As a measure of security. Released March 18, 1809, by order of the general in chief.

117. Miguel de los Rios. Spanish mulatto. February 19, 1809. As a measure of security. Released March 18, 1809, by order of the general in chief.

118. Juan Liseria. Spanish mulatto. February 19, 1809. As a measure of security. Released March 18, 1809, by order of the general in chief.

119. José Torres. Spanish mulatto. February 19, 1809. As a measure of security. Released March 16, 1809, by orders of the general in chief.

120. Simón Figueroa. Spanish mulatto. February 19, 1809. As a measure of security. Released March 16, 1809, by order of the general in chief.

121. Francisco del Rosario. Spanish mulatto. February 19, 1809. As a measure of security. Released March 17, 1809, by order of the general in chief.

122. Jasinto Sanchez. Spanish mulatto. February 19, 1809. As a measure of security. Released March 16, 1809, by order of the general in chief.

123. Felipe Suaro. Spanish mulatto. February 19, 1809. As a measure of security. No release date provided.

124. Bernardino Brisa. Spanish mulatto. February 19, 1809. As a measure of security. Released March 14, 1809, by order of the general in chief.

125. Juan Sanchez. Spanish mulatto. February 19, 1809. As a measure of security. Released March 16, 1809 by order of the general in chief.

126. Gerónimo Rivera. Spanish mulatto. February 19, 1809. As a measure of security. Released March 18, 1809 by order of the general in chief..

127. Juan de Quesada. Spanish mulatto. February 19, 1809. As a measure of security. Released March 18, 1809, by order of the general in chief.

128. Pedro Visioso. Spanish mulatto. February 19, 1809. As a measure of security. Released March 20, 1809, by order of the general in chief.

129. Fernando Sánchez. Spanish mulatto. February 19, 1809. As a measure of security. Released March 16, 1809, by order of the general in chief.

130. Serpentino. Spanish mulatto. February 19, 1809. As a measure of security. Released March 15, 1809, by order of the general in chief.

131. Juan de la Trucha. Spanish mulatto. February 19, 1809. As a measure of security. Released by order of the general in chief.

132. Gregorio de Castro. Spanish mulatto. February 19, 1809. As a measure of security. Sent aboard the privateer *La Bonne Nouvelle* April 27, 1809, by orders of the general in chief.

133. Baltasar Salazar. Spanish mulatto. February 19, 1809. As a measure of security. Sent aboard the privateer *La Bonne Nouvelle* April 27, 1809, by order of the general in chief.

134. Pedro Sianca. Spanish mulatto. February 19, 1809. As a measure of security. Sent aboard the privateer *La Bonne Nouvelle* April 27, 1809, by order of the general in chief.

135. Manuel Aguero. Spanish mulatto. February 19, 1809. As a measure of security. Released March 10, 1809, by order of the general in chief.

136. Antonio Blanco. Spanish mulatto. February 19, 1809. As a measure of security. Released March 8, 1809, by order of the general in chief.

137. Marcelo Calderón. Spanish mulatto. February 19, 1809. As a measure of security. Died in prison March 3, 1809.

138. José de León. Spanish mulatto. February 19, 1809. As a measure of security. Sent aboard the privateer *La Bonne Nouvelle* April 27, 1809, by order of the general in chief.

139. Felis Ramirez. Spanish mulatto. February 19, 1809. As a measure of security. Sent aboard the privateer *La Bonne Nouvelle* April 27, 1809, by order of the general in chief.

140. José Pérez. Spanish mulatto. February 19, 1809. As a measure of security. Released March 13, 1809, by order of the general in chief.

141. Francisco de la Cruz. Spanish mulatto. February 19, 1809. As a measure of security. Chose to embark on the privateer *Bonne Nouvelle* April 27, 1809, by order of the general in chief.

142. Joaquín Ximenez. Spanish mulatto. February 19, 1809. As a measure of secuiity. Released March 20, 1809, by order of the general in chief.

143. Julián Cordero. Spanish mulatto. February 19, 1809. As a measure of security. Released March 17, 1809, by order of the general in chief.

144. Pedro Figueroa. Spanish mulatto. February 19, 1809. As a measure of security. Released April 6, 1809, by order of the general in chief.

145. Francisco Xavier. Spanish mulatto. February 19, 1809. As a measure of security. Released March 15, 1809, by order of the general in chief.

146. Pedro García. Spanish mulatto. February 19, 1809. As a measure of security. Released April 4, 1809, by order of the general in chief.

147. Juan Sedeno. Spanish mulatto. February 19, 1809. As a measure of security. Released March 18, 1809, by order of the general in chief.

148. Bentura Perdomo. Spanish mulatto. February 19, 1809. As a measure of security. Released March 16, 1809, by order of the general in chief.

149. Manuel Hermosa. Spanish mulatto. Februry 19, 1809. As a measure of security. Released March 18, 1809, by order of the general in chief.

150. José Ramírez. Black Spaniard. February 19, 1809. As a measure of security. Released March 23, 1809, by order of the general in chief.

151. Nicolás Romero. Black Spaniard. February 19, 1809. As a measure of security. Released March 18, 1809, by order of the general in chief.

152. Juan Miguel Ramos. Black Spaniard. February 19, 1809. As a measure of security. Released April 15, 1809, by order of the general in chief.

153. Eusebio del Rosario. Black Spaniard. February 19, 1809. As a measure of security. Died in prison March 23, 1809.

154. Manuel Gros. Black Spaniard. February 19, 1809. As a measure of security. Escaped from the public works April 8, 1809.

155. José Nuñez. Black Spaniard. February 19, 1809. As a measure of security. Released March 16, 1809, by orders of the general in chief.

156. Ricardo de la Parra. Black Spaniard. February 19, 1809. As a measure of security. Chose to embark on the privateer *La Bonne Nouvelle* April 27, 1809, by order of the general in chief.

157. José Fernandez. Black Spaniard. February 20, 1809. As a measure of security. Died in prison March 1, 1809.

158. Francisco Mathias. Spanish mulatto. February 21, 1809. As a measure of security. Released March 14, 1809, by order of the general in chief.

159. Manuel Garcia. Spanish mulatto. February 21, 1809. As a measure of security. Released March 16, 1809, by order of the general in chief.

160. José Chavarria. Spanish mulatto. February 21, 1809. As a measure of security. Released March 4, 1809, by order of the general in chief.

161. José Robles. Spanish mulatto. February 21, 1809. As a measure of security. Released March 18, 1809, by order of the general in chief.

162. Manso Polanco. Black Spaniard. February 21, 1809. As a measure of security. Released March 18, 1809, by order of the general in chief.

163. Nicolas Felix. February 21, 1809. Black Spaniard. As a measure of security. Died in prison April 21, 1809.

164. José Medina. Black Spaniard. February 24, 1809. As a measure of security. Released March 10, 1809, by order of the general in chief.

165. José Cavallero. Black Spaniard. February 23, 1809. As a measure of security. Released March 10, 1809, by order of the general in chief.

166. Manuel Garcia. Black Spaniard. February 23, 1809. As a measure of security. [No release date noted.]

167. Damián González. Spanish mulatto. February 23, 1809. As a measure of security. Chose to embark on the privateer *La Bonne Nouvelle* April 27, 1809, by order of the general in chief.

168. Nicolas. Black Spaniard. February 23, 1809. As a measure of security. Released March 17, 1809, by order of the general in chief.

169. Ramon Valverde. White Spaniard. February 24, 1809. As a measure of security. Released March 14, 1809, by order of the general in chief.

170. Miguel Cepeda. White Spaniard. February 24, 1809. As a measure of security. Released March 16, 1809, by order of the general in chief.

171. Domingo Peltuño. White Spaniard. February 24, 1809. As a measure of security. Released March 12, 1809, by order of the general in chief.

172. Rafael Aponte. White Spaniard. February 24, 1809. As a measure of security. Released March 16, 1809, by order of the general in chief.

173. Antonio Acevedo. White Spaniard. February 24, 1809. As a measure of security. Released March 18, 1809, by order of the general in chief.

174. José Orboyal. White Spaniard. February 24, 1809. As a measure of security. Released April 13, 1809, by order of the general in chief.

175. Juan Achete. White Spaniard. February 24, 1809. As a measure of security. Released March 16, 1809, by order of the general in chief.

176. Miguel Fino. Spanish mulatto. February 24, 1809. As a measure of security. Released March 16, 1809, by order of the general in chief.

177. Lorenzo Rodríguez. Spanish mulatto. February 26, 1809. As a measure of security. Released March 16, 1809, by order of the general in chief.

178. Manuel Hermoso. Spanish mulatto. February 26, 1809. As a measure of security. Released March 6, 1809, by order of the general in chief.

179. José del Rosario. Spanish mulatto. February 26, 1809. As a measure of security. Released March 10, 1809, by order of the heneral in chief.

180. José Nuñez. White Spaniard. March 3, 1809. As a measure of security. Released March 13, 1809, by order of the general in chief.

181. José Selidon. Black Spaniard. March 4, 1809. As a measure of security. Released March 18, 1809, by order of the general in chief.

182. Eusebio Nuñez. Spanish mulatto. March 5, 1809. As a measure of security. Died in prison April 6, 1809.

183. José de Loado. Spanish mulatto. March 5, 1809. As a measure of security. Released March 18, 1809, by order of the general in chief.

184. Juan Diego. Spanish mulatto. March 5, 1809. As a measure of security. Released March 6, 1809.

185. José Pérez. Spanish mulatto. March 5, 1809. As a measure of security. Released March 7, 1809, by order of the general in chief.

186. Manuel Nolasco. Spanish mulatto. March 5, 1809, As a measure of security. Released March 18, 1809.

187. Pedro Martines. Spanish mulatto. March 5, 1809. As a measure of security. Released March 18, 1809.

188. Simon. Black Englishman. March 5, 1809. As a measure of security. Died in prison March 20, 1809.

189. Jean Louis. Black Frenchman. March 6, 1809. As a measure of security. Released March 15, 1809, by order of the commander of the army.

190. José Ximenes. White Spaniard. March 8, 1809. As a measure of security. Released March 18, 1809, by order of the general in chief.

191. Letronier. White Frenchman. March 8, 1809. As a measure of security. Released March 16, 1809, by order of the commander of the army.

192. Santiago Ramíre. Black Spaniard, belongs to Letronier. March 9, 1809. As a measure of security. Died in prison March 26, 1809.

193. José Mella. Spanish mulatto, belongs to Letronier. March 9, 1809. As a measure of security. Released March 18, 1809, by order of the commander of the army.

194. Pedro Mella. Spanish mulatto, belongs to Letronier. March 9, 1809. As a measure of security. Released March 18, 1809, by order of the commander of the army.

195. Marion. White Frenchman. March 10, 1809. Arrested by superior order. Released March 17, 1809, by order of the commander of the army.

196. Agustín Espinosa. White Spaniard. March 10, 1809. As a measure of security. Died in prison April 6, 1809.

197. Juan de Mella. Spanish mulatto. March 10, 1809. As a measure of security. Released March 18, 1809, by order of the commander of the army.

198. Agustín Camareno. Black Spaniard. March 10, 1809. As a measure of security. Escaped from the public works April 2, 1809.

199. Pablo de Quesada. Spanish mulatto. March 10, 1809. As a measure of security. Released March 29, 1809, by order of the commander of the army.

200. Miguel Indio. Spanish mulatto. March 10, 1809. As a measure of security. Died in prison May 9, 1809.

201. Serapio Fereyro. Spanish mulatto. March 11, 1809. As a measure of security. Released May 28, 1809, by order of the commander of the army.

202. Carlos Colon. Spanish mulatto. March 11, 1809. As a measure of security. No release date given.

203. Manuel Velasco. Spanish mulatto. March 11, 1809. As a measure of security. Released March 13, 1809, by order of the commander of the army.

204. Juan Ramírez. Spanish mulatto. March 11, 1809. As a measure of security. Released March 11, 1809. Double entry.

205. Francisco Llanes. Black Spanish. March 11, 1809. As a measure of security. No release date noted.

206. Antonio Cueto. Spanish mulatto. March 11, 1809. As a measure of security. Released April 26, 1809, by order of the commander of the army.

207. Ramón Pérez. Spanish mulatto. March 11, 1809. As a measure of security. Released March 15, 1809, by order of the commander of the army.

208. Juan Diego. Spanish mulatto. March 11, 1809. As a measure of security. Date of release omitted.

209. Juan Ramírez. Black Spaniard. March 11, 1809. As a measure of security. Released March 18, 1809, by order of the commander of the army.

210. Francisco Nolasco. Black Spaniard. March 11, 1809. As a measure of security. Released March 18, 1809, by order of the commander of the army.

211. Agustín Ravelo. Spanish mulatto. March 11, 1809. As a measure of security. Released April 13, 1809, by order of the general in chief.

212. Manuel Girod. Spanish mulatto. March 11, 1809. As a measure of security. Released April 13, 1809, by order of the general in chief.

213. Louis Miranda. Black Spaniard. March 11, 1809. As a measure of security. Died in prison April 25, 1809.

214. Francisco Guante. Black Spaniard. March 11, 1809. As a measure of security. Released March 21, 1809, by order of the commander of the army.

215. Lefebvre. White Frenchman. March 11, 1809. Rifleman of the 5th Regiment, as a measure of security. Escaped prison April 9, 1809.

216. Gonzal. Spanish mulatto. Colonial scout. March 11, 1809. As a measure of security. Released April 13, 1809, by order of the general in chief.

217. Barotte. White Frenchman, ex-concierge of Artillery residence.

March 15, 1809. The Spaniards made him contribute. As a measure of security. Released June 11, 1809, by order of the general in chief.

218. Lassere. White Frenchman. March 24, 1809. As a measure of security and for having seditious papers against superior officers. Released April 10, 1809, by order of the commander of the army.

219. Grégoire. Black Spanish Boy. March 25, 1809. As a measure of security. Released April 4, 1809, by order of the commander of the army.

220. Lucile. Black French. April 9, 1809. As a measure of security. Released April 1, 1809, by order of the general in chief.

231. Barthélemy. French Black belonging to M. Cadet Montes. April 18, 1809. As a measure of security. Released April 22, 1809, by request of Colonel Refussaud, by order of the general in chief.

232. Carlos Justo. Spanish mulatto. April 21, 1809. Arrested by the commissary of police, as a measure of security. Died in prison May 25, 1809.

233. Gravier Maldonado. Spanish mulatto. April 23, 1809. Arrested by the ommissary of olice, as a measure of security. Died in prison June 17, 1809.

234. Manuel. Black Spaniard. A slave. April 28, 1809. For having had seditious intentions. Released April 30, 1809, by order of the commander of the army.

235. Francisco Madrigal. White Spaniard. May 8, 1809. As a measure of security. No release date given.

236. Catherine. Black French. May 8, 1809. Arrested as a measure of security by the ommissary of olice. Released May 9, 1809, by order of the commander of the army.

237. Franchette. Black French. May 10, 1809. As a measure of security. Died in prison June 6, 1809.

238. Juan de Acevedo. White Spaniard. May 13, 1809. As a measure of security. Released June 30, 1809, by commander of the army.

239. Manuel Ramírez. White Spaniard. May 16, 1809. Released July 9, 1809, by general in chief.

240. Francise. French mulatto. May 23, 1809. As a measure of security. Released May 30, 1809, by order of the commander of the army.

241. Manuela. White Spaniard. June 1, 1809. As a measure of security. Released June 23, 1809, by order of the commander of the army.

242. Chevery. White Frenchman. June 4, 1809. As a measure of security. Released June 11, 1809, by order of the commander of the army.

243. Pauline Sterlin. French mulatto. June 4, 1809. As a measure of security. Released June 21, 1809, by order of the general in chief.

244. Rose. French mulatto. June 5, 1809. As a measure of security. Released June 21, 1809, by order of the general in chief.

APPENDIX 2

Dominican Soldiers and Sailors Captured by the French in Action at the Siege of Santo Domingo, 1809

1. José Figueroa. Spanish mulatto. January 5, 1809. Made a prisoner by a rifleman of the Colonial Legion in yesterday's combat at Saint-Charles. Released March 12, 1809, to be exchanged, by order of the general in chief.

2. Juan González. Spanish mulatto. January 24, 1809. Resident of San Juan made prisoner by the column commanded by Colonel Vassinou today. Died in prison January 28, 1809.

3. Thomas Vilorio. Spanish mulatto. January 24, 1809. Resident of San Juan. Captured as above. Released March 12, 1809, to be exchanged.

4. Thomas Peralta. Spanish mulatto. January 24, 1809. Resident of San Juan. Captured as above. Released March 12, 1809, to be exchanged.

5. Francisco García. Spanish mulatto. January 24, 1809. Resident of San Juan. Captured and released as above.

6. Ramón Moreno. Spanish mulatto. January 24, 1809. Resident of San Juan. Captured and released as above.

7. Damián González. Spanish mulatto. January 24, 1809. Resident of San Juan. Captured and released as above.

8. Martin del Rosario. Black Spaniard. January 24, 1809. Resident of Azua. Captured and released as above.

Note: Names transcribed according to the following source: CC 9 a 45, "Registre des prisonniers (civil) an XIV-1809."

9. Domingo de Paula. Spanish mulatto. January 24, 1809. Resident of Azua. Captured and released as above.

10. Juan Polar. Spanish mulatto. January 24, 1809. Resident of Azua. Captured and released above.

11. Silvestre Franco. Spanish mulatto. January 24, 1809. Resident of Azua. Captured and released as above.

12. Juan de Padua. Spanish mulatto. January 24, 1809. Resident of Azua. Captured and released as above.

13. Ignacio Caravallo. Spanish mulatto. January 24, 1809. Resident of Azua. Captured and released as above.

14. Marcelino de Lion. Spanish mulatto. January 24, 1809. Resident of Santo Domingo. Captured and released as above.

15. José Haque. Black Spaniard. January 24, 1809. Resident of Cotuí. Captured and released as above.

16. Pedro Villa. Spanish mulatto. January 24, 1809. Resident of Cotuí. Captured and released as above.

17. Leon Sanchez. Spanish mulatto. January 24, 1809. Resident of Cotui. Captured and released as above.

18. Domingo Galan. Spanish mulatto. January 24, 1809. Resident o Cotui. Captured and released as above.

19. Gregorio Serrano. Spanish mulatto. January 24, 1809. Resident of Cotuí. Captured and released as above.

20. Ignosensio Sanchez. Spanish mulatto. January 24, 1809. Resident of Cotuí. Captured and released as above.

21. José Gonzalez. Spanish mulatto. January 24, 1809. Resident of Cotuí. Captured and released as above.

22. Manuel de Luna. Spanish mulatto. Janaury 24, 1809. Resident of Cotuí. Captured and released as above.

23. Martines Martes. Spaniosh mulatto. January 24, 1809. Resident of Cotuí. Captured and released as above.

24. Thomas Varder. Spanish mulatto. January 24, 1809. Resident of Banica. Captured and released as above.

25. Manuel Soriano. Black Spaniard. January 24, 1809. Resident of Banica. Captured and released as above.

26. Juan Crisostomo. Spanish mulatto. January 24, 1809. Resident of Hayna. Captured and released as above.

27. Manuel Camarena. Spanish mulatto. January 24, 1809. Resident of Santiago. Captured as above, he died in prison on February 14, 1809.

28. Manuel Rudesindo. Spanish mulatto. January 24, 1809. Resident of Santiago. Captured and released as above.

29. Santiago Pitré. Spanish mulatto. January 24, 1809. Resident of Ceybo. Captured and released as above.

30. Mundo Santa Ana. Spanish mulatto. January 24, 1809. Resident of Ceybo. Captured and released as above.

31. José Dias. Black Spaniard. January 27, 1809. Resident of San Juan, he was made a prisoner in the sortie of December 5, 1808, and he was in the hospital. Released March 12, 1809, to be exchanged.

32. Phelipe Suaria. February 2, 1809. Made prisoner on January 5, he was at the hospital. Released March 12, 1809, to be exchanged.

33. Noverto Sierra. Black Spaniard. February 9, 1809. Resident of Los Ingenios, made prisoner of war on January 24, 1809, he was in the hospital for wounds. Released March 12, 1809, to be exchanged.

34. Geronimo Bello. White Spaniard. February 13, 1809. Regular gunner, he was madde prisoner. Released March 12, 1809, to be exchanged.

35. Juan Figueroa. Spanish mulatto. February 13, 1809. Inhabitant of Samaná. Regular gunner, made prisoner, released March 12, 1809, to be exchanged.

36. Antonio José. White Spaniard. May 6, 1809. Sailor of the English schooner *William* captured by the French ship *La Supérieure*. No release date given.

37. Bisente Cemboro. White Spaniard. May 6, 1809. Same as above.

38. Ramón Guante. White Spaniard. May 6, 1809. Same as above.

39. Manuel Gonzalez. White Spaniard. May 6, 1809. Same as above.

APPENDIX 3

Soldiers of the Puerto Rican Fixed Regiment Made Prisoner in Action against the French during the Siege of Santo Domingo, 1809

1. Matheo Valdivieso. White Spaniard. January 24, 1809. Corporal of grenadiers of the Fixed Regiment of Puerto Rico, made prisoner by the column commanded by Colonel Vassinou today. Released March 12, 1809, to be exchanged by order of the general in chief.

2. Salvador Oviedo. White Spaniard. January 24, 1809. Grenadier. Captured and exchanged as above.

3. José de Castro. White Spaniard. January 24 1809. Grenadier. Captured and exchanged as above.

4. José Rodríguez. White Spaniard. January 24, 1809. Grenadier. Captured and exchanged as above.

5. José Dabila. White Spaniard. January 24, 1809. Grenadier. Captured and exchanged as above.

6. Romaldo Urbina. White Spaniard. January 24 1809. Grenadier. Captured and exchanged as above.

7. Manuel Rueda. White Spaniard. January 24, 1809. Fusilier. Captured and exchanged as above.

8. Diego Rodríguez. White Spaniard. January 24, 1809. Fusilier. Captured and exchanged as above.

9. José Rueda. White Spaniard. Janaury 24, 1809. Fusilier. Captured and exchanged as above.

10. Bernardino Ramires. White Spaniard. January 24, 1809. Fusilier. Captured and exchanged as above.

11. Francisco de Laura. White Spaniard. January 24, 1809. Fusilier. Captured and exchanged as above.

Notes

Chapter 1

1. See Godechot, *France and the Atlantic Revolution of the Eighteenth Century, 1770–1799*; Palmer, *The Age of the Democratic Revolution*.
2. British-ruled Quebec, Newfoundland, Bermuda, and Florida did not join the thirteen rebel colonies.
3. Langley, *The Americas in the Age of Revolution, 1750–1850*.
4. It would be good to recall Ivan Illich's views on the subject. Ivan Illich, *En América ¿Para qué sirve la escuela?* (Buenos Aires: Ediciones Búsqueda, 1974)
5. Eugène-Edouard Boyer-Peyreleau, *Les Antilles Françaises particulièrement la Guadeloupe depuis leur découverte jusqúau le 1er janvier 1823* (Paris: Librairie de Brissot-Thivans, 1823), 1:291–299; Luis A. Salivia, *Historia de los huracanes y temporales de las Antillas* (San Juan: Editorial Edil, 1972), 113–119.
6. Rivera (comp.), *Circulares de Don Toribio Montes*, no. 69, p. 80; Salivia, op. cit., 129.
7. Rivera, op. cit., no. 101, p. 110.
8. Honychurch, *The Dominica Story*, 117–121 and 270.
9. Boyer de Peyreleau, op. cit., 1:172–173.
10. Duncan, *A Brief History of Saint Vincent*, xiv.
11. Thésée, *Négociants bordelais et colons de Saint-Domingue*, 49.
12. Higman, *Slave Population and Economy in Jamaica, 1807–1834*, 11.
13. Deive, *Las emigraciones dominicanas a Cuba (1795–1808)*, 62.
14. Goslinga, *A Short History of the Netherlands Antilles and Surinam*, 20–25; see Ramón Aizpurrua, *Curazao y la costa de Caracas*.
15. Lowes, *The Peculiar Class*, 128.
16. Humboldt, *Ensayo político sobre la isla de Cuba*, 171.
17. Lavoie, Mayer, and Flick, "A Particular Study of Slavery in the Caribbean Island of Saint-Barthelemy, 1648–1845."
18. Beckles, *A History of Barbados*, 75.
19. See Hall, *The Danish West Indies*.
20. Davis, *The Problem of Slavery in the Age of Revolution, 1770–1823*.
21. See Thompson, *Flight to Freedom*.
22. Sherlock and Bennett, *The Story of the Jamaican People*, 128–148). One impressed observer of the maroon community in Jamaica was the French émigré Moreau de Saint Mery, who wrote in the 1790s that the maroons were strong enough "to come from time to time to massacre the white planters in their proximity and to intimidate whites to such an extreme that they do not dare to distance themselves from the coast" (AN, Colonies Moreau de Saint Mery, F 3/23).
23. See Villaverde, *Diario del Rancheador*.
24. Gaspar, *Bondsmen and Rebels*, 203–204.
25. See Frostin, *Les revoltes blanches a Saint-Domingue aux XVII et XVIIIe siècles*.
26. Robin Blackburn, *The Overthrow of Colonial Slavery, 1776–1848* (London and New York: Verso, 1988), 232.
27. Goslinga, op. cit., 65.
28. Lowe, *The Codrington Correspondence*, 5–6.
29. See Manning, *British Colonial Government after the American Revolution 1783–1820*.

30. Moreta Castillo, *La Real Audiencia de Santo Domingo.*
31. See Bumsted (ed.), *The Great Awakening.*
32. Duncan, *A Brief History of Saint Vincent,* 9.
33. Honychurch, op. cit., 181.
34. Beckles, op. cit., 88–89.
35. See C.O.A. Oldendorp, *History of the Mission of the Evangelical Brethren on the Caribbean Islands of St. Thomas, St. Croix and St. John,* ed. Johan Jakob Bossard, trans. Arnold R. Highfield and Vladimir Barac (Ann Arbor, MI: Karoma Publishers, 1987).
36. Delisle, *Renouveau missionaire et société esclavagiste,* 353.
37. See Picó, "Iglesia y esclavitud en el Caribe hispano."
38. See Emmanuel, *History of the Jews of the Netherlands Antilles.*
39. Alvarez Nazario, "El papiamento: ojeada a su pasado histórico y visión de su problemática de presente"; Emmanuel, op. cit., 1:482.
40. Aceto, "Statian Creole English."
41. Liverpool, *The History and Development of the Saint Lucia Civil Code,* 22.
42. Cox, *Free Colored in the Slave Societies of St. Kitts and Grenada, 1763–1833,* 95.
43. Emmanuel, op. cit., 1:439.
44. Ibid., 144.

Chapter 2

1. Grasso, *A Speaking Aristocracy,* 2ff.
2. See Unger, *John Hancock.*
3. Namier, *England in the Age of the American Revolution.*
4. See, among others, Fruchtman, *Atlantic Cousins.*
5. For the complex financial system used by the French monarchy and the futile efforts to reform it, see Bosher, *French Finances, 1770–1795.*
6. Whitridge, *Rochambeau,* 60–63.
7. Ibid., 68.
8. Bonsal, *When the French Were Here,* 6–7.
9. See Morgan, *"The Pivot Upon Which Everything Turned"; Journal of the Siege of Yorktown.*
10. Goslinga, op. cit., 64.
11. Ibid., 67, 74–75; Emmanuel, op. cit., 1:279–280.
12. See Toth (ed.), *The American Revolution and the West Indies.*
13. See Deive, *Tangomangos;* Peña Pérez, *Antonio Osorio.*
14. A full discussion of these points is found in Rodigneaux, *La guerre de course en Guadeloupe XVIIIe–XIXe siècles,* 25–43. See also Patton, *Patriot Pirates.* Historians of pirates and privateers tend to forget that the Iberian Peninsula had its own tradition of piracy, which went back to the Basques in the fourteenth century in the Bay of Biscay. In the Caribbean there were prominent cases of privateers from the Spanish islands, like Miguel Enríquez, whom Philip V named Caballero de la Real Efigie (see López Cantos, *Miguel Enríquez.*
15. See Thésée, op. cit.
16. Ott, *The Haitian Revolution, 1789–1804,* 8.
17. See Frostin, op. cit.
18. For a discussion of these matters, see Nelson, "Making Men."
19. Carolyn Fick, "The French Revolution in Saint-Domingue, A Triumph or a Failure?" in Gaspar and Geggus (eds.), *A Turbulent Time,* 55–56.
20. Griggs and Prator (eds.), *Henry Christophe and Thomas Clarkson,* 10.
21. *Cahier, contenant les plaintes, doleances and reclamations,* p. 1, art. 1.
22. Griggs and Prator, op. cit., 12.
23. Ott, op. cit., 39.
24. Ibid., 57–58.
25. Fick, "The French Revolution," in Gaspar and Geggus, op. cit., 70.
26. Blackburn, *Overthrow of Colonial Slavery,* 197.

27. Deive, *Los Guerrilleros Negros*, 203–212.
28. Blackburn, op. cit., 217.
29. Ott, op. cit., 82.
30. Blackburn, op. cit., 228–233.
31. Incháustegui, *Documentos para Estudio*, 1:49–50.
32. Deive, *Las emigraciones dominicanas a Cuba*, 31; Jane C. Landers, "Revolt and Royalism in Spanish Florida: The French Revolution on Spain's Northern Colonial Frontier," in Gaspar and Geggus, op. cit., 161–169.
33. "Constitution de la Colonie Française de Saint-Domingue envoyée au Premier Consul, par Toussaint Louverture," Titre VIII, Du Gouvernement. Text published in Peyre-Ferry, *Journal des operations militaires de l'Armée Française a Saint-Domingue*, 365.
34. Peyre-Ferry, op. cit., 53.
35. Shortly after his arrival, on February 15, 1802, he told some officers of the Rochambeau division that it would take two months: "que nous avions encore deux mois avant que les chaleurs fussent insupportables, et qu'il espérait qu'avant cette époque, la campagne serait terminée" (ibid., 60).
36. Miranda, *The New Democracy in America*.
37. David Patrick Geggus, "Slavery, War and Revolution in the Greater Caribbean 1789–1815," in Gaspar and Geggus, op. cit., 14.
38. Michael Duffy, "The French Revolution and British Attitudes to the West Indian Colonies," in Gaspar and Geggus, op. cit., 87ff.; Geggus, *Slavery, War and Revolution*, 387.
39. Arcaya, *Insurrección de los Negros de la Serranía de Coro*, 41–56.
40. Ibid., 13–38; Grafenstein García, *Nueva España en el Circumcaribe 1779–1808*, 252.
41. Honychurch, op. cit., 102–103.
42. See Reed, *The American, French, Haitian and Spanish American Revolutions, 1775–1825*, 70–72.
43. See Trouillot, *Nation, State and Society in Haiti, 1804–1984*, 9–11.
44. Grafenstein García, op. cit., 280. The reference to the authors cited is "Die Grosse Frucht in der Karibik: Frankreich, Saint-Domingue und Kuba, 1789–1795," *Iberoamerikanisch Archiv* 17, no. 1 (1991).
45. Rivera, op. cit., no. 37.
46. Ibid., no. 41 (A), pp. 55–56.
47. Ibid., no. 44, p. 59.
48. Ibid., no. 110.
49. Grafenstein García, op. cit., 251–252.

Chapter 3

1. *Dictionnaire de Biographie Française*, s.v. "Ferrand, Jean Louis" (by H. Duchêne-Marullaz). Another birth date given is October 12, 1753 ("Ferrand, Marie Louis," http://famousamericans.net).
2. See *Dictionnaire de Biographie Française*.
3. See FamousAmericans.net.
4. Ibid.
5. See Peyre-Ferry, *Journal des opérations militaires de l'Armée Française à Saint-Domingue*.
6. Archives Nationales (hereafter cited as AN), Colonies, CC 9 a 40, "Copie de la Correspondance du General Ferrand," cahier 1, 28 Frimaire an 12, missive to Dubarquier (hereafter cited as "Correspondance Ferrand").
7. AN, CC 9 a 44, nominations to the Legion of Honor submitted by Ferrand, "Légion d'honneur, Saint Domingue," 1 r.
8. Portal de Archivos Españoles (hereafter cited as PARES), Archivo General de Simancas, legajo 7154, expediente 14, 131 r–134 r; legajo 7156, expediente 96, 303 r; legajo 7182, expediente 35, 155 r–158 r.

9. PARES, Archivo General de Indias, Estado, legajo 4 no. 5, "Minuta de oficio a Manuel de Peralta."

10. "Correspondance Ferrand," CC 9 a 40, cahier 2, 5 Pluviose an 12.

11. Ibid., 16 Pluviose an 12.

12. Ibid., cahier 1, 8 Nivose an 12.

13. Ibid., cahier 2, 30 Nivose an 12: "ne comptez-vous pour rien la honte de vivre sous les ordres des hommes que furent vos esclaves."

14. Ibid., cahier 3, 25 Pluviose an 12: "Je compte sur vous, citoyen commandant, pour me seconder ainsi que le commandant Ruiz, dans nos intentions bien prononcées de contribuer au Bonheur des habitants de la cidevant partie espagnole tout en nous occupant des interets du gouvernemene que nous servions."

15. Ibid., cahier 19, Ferrand to González, resident in Azúa, 19 Floreal an 13. Around that time there is another letter from Ferrand to señores González, Mateo, Jiménez, and Felix, residents of Azúa, to have them assemble the principal residents of the district to nominate a new commandant.

16. Ibid., CC 9 a 45, Correspondance a l'Interieur, cahier 3, June 10, 1808; cahier 5, October 23, 1808.

17. Ibid., CC 9 a 40, cahier 9, 26 Prairial an 12.

18. Ibid., cahier 10, 15 Messidor an 12.

19. Ibid., cahier 11, 8 Thermidor an 12.

20. Ibid., cahier 20, 23 Floreal an 13.

21. Ibid., cahier 15, 23 Frimaire an 13.

22. Ibid., CC 9 a 45, Correspondance a l'Interieur, cahier 1, February 22, 1808.

23. Ibid., March 14, 1808.

24. Ibid., cahier 2, April 3, 1808, Ferrand to Barquier.

25. See Rodigneaux, *La Guerre de Course en Guadeloupe*; see also Patton, *Patriot Pirates*.

26. Robin Blackburn, *The Overthrow of Colonial Slavery* 227; Boyer-Peyrleau, *Les Antilles Françaises particulièrement la Guadeloupe*, vol. 2, app. 11. There is some correspondence on the privateers from Guadeloupe who brought their prizes to Puerto Rico in Archivo General de Puerto Rico (hereafter cited as AGPR), FGEPR, box 28.

27. Some of the correspondence on the privateers licensed by Sonthonax is found in a collection of letters received by Sonthonax in Bibliothèque Nationale de la France, Ms Nouvelles Acquisitions Françaises 6846.

28. See Ferrand's communications to the minister of marine and colonies on 13 Thermidor an 12 (CC 9 a 40, cahier 11).

29. CC 9 a 40, cahier 20, 19 Floreal an 13. In a message to Congress in 1806, President Thomas Jefferson strongly protested French interception of American ships in the waters of Haiti.

30. Ibid., cahier 12, 3 Vendimiare an 13, "Arreté qui ordonna la remise du Brick La Zuanne."

31. Ibid., cahier 4, 7 Ventose an 12.

32. See Archbishop Fernando Portillo's circular to the clergy in Rodríguez Demorizi, *La Era de Francia en Santo Domingo*, 22 s; Deive, *Las emigraciones dominicanas a Cuba*, 51–52.

33. CC 9 a 40, cahier 1, 23 Nivose an 12.

34. See, e.g., Ferrand's communication to the minister of the public treasury on 1 Ventose an 12 (CC 9 a 40, cahier 4).

35. CC 9 a 40, cahier 17, 22 Pluviose an 13, Ferrand to the count of Matenfels. See also his communication to the governor of Curaçao, ibid., cahier 14, 30 Brumaire an 13.

36. Ibid., cahier 17, 8 Ventose an 13: "Quoique je suis convaincu qu'ils n'arriveront pas jusqu'a Santo Domingo, nous ne devons pas cependant rien négliger, pour n'etre pas pris au depourvu, et je vous demande la plus grande celerité, pour toutes les dispositions qu'exige la defense de la place dont le Commandement vous est confié."

37. Ibid., 11 Ventose an 13.

38. Ibid., 13 Ventose an 13.

39. Ibid., 15 Ventose an 13.

40. Ibid., cahier 18, 16 Ventose an 13.

41. Ibid., 18 Ventose an 13: "Dessalines est aux portes de Santo Domingo, avec dic mille hommes. J'ai lieu de croire que je conserverai la place assez de tems [*sic*], pour le dégouter de cette enterprise, et que cet événement finira para etre avantageux au Gouvernement, mais il nous faut de vivres et quelques hommes."

42. Ibid.

43. Ibid., 20 Ventose an 13.

44. Ibid., 25 Venrose an 13.

45. Ibid., 28 Ventose an 13: "Les brigands sont toujours sous les murs, et j'ai lieu de croire qu'ils seront plutot degoutés que nous, d'un siege qu'ils n'avoient pas prevu aussi difficile."

46. Ibid., 29 Ventose an 13: "Outre l'avanatage de nuir aux négres, je trouve dans cette opération celui d'approvisioner la place, et celle mesure sera ajoutée, a toute celles que j'ai prise a cet égard. Au rest, pour plus amples instructions, donnez vous la peine de passer chez moi dans la journée avec Pagard."

47. Ibid., 7 Germinal an 13: "Depuis le 15 Ventose dernier les negres revoltés m'assiégent dans la place de Santo Domingo avec une armée de huit mille hommes de leurs meilleurs troupes, commandés para Clervaux, Christophe, Pétion et Jean Philippe Dan. Ils sont maitres de toute la campagne, et n'ayant plus de communication avec le dehors, je suis par conséquent borné aux faibles moyens qui sont concentrés dans la place, et aux vivres qui m'arrivent de tems en tems par mer, mais qui sont toujours en proportion insuffisant avec mes besoins. Les précautions que j'ai prises des le commencement du siège, de renvoyer la plus grande partie des bouches inutiles de la place, sur les batiments qui se trouvaient dans le port, m'a fourni le double moyen de diminuer ma consommation de vivres, et de ne pas lasser, aux hommes qui craignent, l'espoir et le désir de s'embarquer. Je travaillerai a me maintenir dans la place, avec les moyens que j'ai et ceux que l'Amiral Missiessy et le Géneral Lagrange ont eu la bonté de me fournir, avec beaucopu d'obligeance. Avec l'arrivée du renfort des 550 hommes que Votre Excellence a eu la bonté de m'envoyer, mes forces se bornaent a 800 hommes de ligne et a 1500 hommes a peu près de milices Espagnoles, qui sont sans discipline et sans résolution, la plus grande partie composée de negres, avec les quels ont ne peut rien entreprende de hazardeux ni de decisif. Ma perte depuis le siège par le feu de l'ennemi se porte a une cinquantaine d'hommes. J'ai plus de 60 blessés dans les hopitaux."

48. Ibid., 7 Germinal an 13. "Cela donnerait a penser aux Brigands qui sont devalt la place, et suffisant a leur fire lever le siège."

49. Ibid., 8 Germinal an 13.

50. See Ferrand's requests for help in CC 9 a 40, cahier 18, 16 and 22 Ventose an 13.

51. CC 9 a 45, "Pièces éparses" (extract of an account of Dessalines's death forwarded from Philadelphia).

52. Moya Pons, *La dominación haitiana, 1822–1844*, chap. 1.

53. CC 9 a 45, cahier 6, 19 and 21 Germinal an 13.

54. Ibid., cahier 1, 12 Nivose an 12. In the French garrison, there were not only Poles but also Italians, Swiss, and Germans who for one reason or another had come to form part of Napoleon's armies.

55. Ibid., cahier 3, 1 Ventose an 12, 23 Pluviose an 12.

56. Ibid., cahier 20, 2 Prairial an 13: "Autant que le Géneral entend qu'il y ait de subordination a la parte des inferieurs vis a vis de leur supérieurs, autant il exige d'égard de la part de ceux-ci envers les subordinnés; et il punira légalement les fautes que aureaient lieu dans ces different cas. Le Géneral est informé, qu'il y a souvent des rixes entre les militaires,et il n'ignore pas que ces rixes sont presque toujours l éffet de l'ivresse. Il recommande de plus de sobriété, et prévient qu'il punira séverement les querelleurs. Le Géneral n'entend pas que les Militaires vivent comme des capucins, mas il est possible de s'egayer sans se battre."

57. CC 9 a 43, cahier 25, 27 Nivose an 14.
58. Ibid., February 1, 1806.

Chapter 4

1. See Deive, op. cit.; and Schaeffer, "The Delayed Cession of Spanish Santo Domingo to France, 1795–1801."
2. CC 9 a 40, cahier 2, 1 Pluviose an 12.
3. Ibid., cahier 23, 30 Vendimiare an 14, Ferrand to commander Dorby.
4. Dorvo Soulastre, "Viaje por tierra de Santo Domingo, Capital de la Parte española de Santo Domingo, al Cabo Francés, Capital de la parte francesa de la misma isla," transl. C. Armand Rodríguez, in Rodríguez Demorizi, *La Era de Francia en Santo Domingo,* 89; See *Enciclopedia Dominicana,* vol. 3 (2nd ed. rev.; Santo Domingo, 1978).
5. CC 9 a 40, cahier 3, 22 Pluviose an 12: "Comparez le joug sur le quel vous vivez avec la moderation française, et vous n'hesiterez pas a envoyer a Santo Domingo des officiers avec qui je traitarais, pour vous arracher de la tyrannie de Dessalines. La position de ce brigand, et la notre a Santo Domingo ne peuvent vous laisser un moment incertain."
6. Ibid., cahier 5, 22 Ventose an 12: Je verais avec . . . plaisir que vous en ferez usage pour quitter des lieux que l'honneur vous deffend d'habiter jusquá nouvel ordre."
7. Ibid., cahier 9, 24 Prairial an 12: "Je prens la confiance de vous reccomander particulierment la famille de Mr. Espaillat qui s'embarque ajourd'hui a l'effet de passer a Puerto Rico. Cette famille, ainsi que celles qui sont sur le meme batiment, ont été forcés d'abandonner leur propriété, et ce qu'elles emportent avec elles, fait toute leur fortune. C'est vous dire, mon cher commandant, qu'elles ont des droits a votre humanité, et je suis convaincu, si le hazard metre votre pouvoir sur ces emigrés que vous les traiterez aussi favoreblement que tant de personnes, qui ne cessentd e faire votre éloge."
8. One of his sons, Francisco Antonio, is one of three Dominican migrrants who wrote from Aguadilla on November 29, 1808, to the Supreme Junta in Spain to express support for Juan Sánchez Ramírez (PARES, Archivo Histórico Nacional, Junta Suprema de Estado, legajo 60 C, document 48).
9. CC 9 a 40, cahier 1, 1 Pluviose an 12.
10. Ibid., cahier 5, 26 Ventose an 12: "Citoyens, vous manquez de toute espèce de ressources et la partie de l'Isle de Saint Domingue occupée par les franèais vous en offre de nouvelles. Rentrez dans une Ysle dont vous connaissez tous les avantages, et que ne pouvez cesser de regarder comme votre patrie. C'est a Sto. Domingo que vous etes attendus. Il sera pourvu des logements et a la subsistance des hommes enm etat de porter les armes qui se fixeront a Sto. Domingo. Toutes les personnes qui voudroint habiter la campagne trouveront en s'utilisant les moyens d'exister. Elles seron logées par les soins du Gouvernement, aussi convenablement qu'il sera possible. Il sera donné, aux personnes qui voudront habiter la campagne, des connexions. Elles n'auront qu'a semer et planter, pour obtenir bien au de la de leurs besoins. Elles aurant du Gouvernement toutes les facilités qu'elles pourront désirer a cet effet. Le Gouvernement des colonies voisines ont été invités au nom du Gouvernement franèais de procurer aux anciens habitants de St Domingue les moyens d'arriver a Santo Domingo. Citoyens, je veux n'auriez pas a craindre des évenements pareils a ceux que vous ont forcé de quitter l'Isle de Saint Domingue, et vous serez en état d attendre que la France, après avoir rétabli la tranquillité dans cette isle, vous remitte en possesion de vos propriétés. Vous vivrez sous un Gouvernement paternal, dans un pays ou les vivres sont en abondance et ou la confiance faut tous les jours de nouveaux progrès."
11. CC 9 a 45, Correspondance Interieure II, April 3, 1808.
12. Ibid., "Lettres du général Ferrand," April 29, 1808.
13. Ibid., CC 9 a 40, cahier 4, communications of 6 Ventose an 12.

14. See, e.g., the authorization given to Captain Tood, commanding the American brig *La Sally* to load mahogany in western Santo Domingo (ibid., cahier 17, 3 Ventose an 13.)

15. Ibid., CC 9 a 45, Correspondance Exterieure I, March 2, 1808: "Comme M. Gazan est un des chefs d'une maison de commerce tres estimée, il se propose, sous la protection de V.E., de menager une liaison commerciale entre la Jamaique et Santo Domingo: ce mouvement reciproque ferait entretien par l'echange des objets dont nous aurions besoin, avec les bestiaux, bois d'acajou, de campêche, et autres denrées que nous pouvions fournir, cependant avec la restriction expresse, des articles dont notre état de guerre prohibe, le commerce respectif. Persuadé d'avance, Monsieur l'Amiral que votre Excellence, ne recontrerait aucun inconvénient dans de pareilles relations, j'ai confié, a M. Gazan, une certaine somme en lettres de change, sur les Etats-Unis d'Amérique, dont il est chargé, de faire l'emploi, d'après la sanction que vous croirez devoir donner au projet que j'ai l'honneur de vous présenter. Notre position dans les colonies est different, de ce qu'elle est en Europe, et notre avantage commun nous fait une loi de nos rélacher de cette animosité nationale, que la fatalité a si fort exaltée. Il nous est permis, sans compromettre notre responsabilité, de nous livrer aux ménagements et a l'impulsion de l'estime naturelle dont la guerre ne devrait jamais proscrire les convenances. La correspondance amicaale que vous avez bien voulu entretenir avec moi, me fait croire, que V.E. partagera une maniere de voir et des principes, qui ne blessent en rien notre honneur ni l'interet de nos souverains."

16. Ibid., "Arretés et décisions des généraux Ferrand puis Barquier 1808–1809," Spanish translation of the police ordinance enacted by the municipal council and signed by Ferrand in February of 1808.

17. Ibid., CC 8 a 40, cahier 21, 8 Messidor an 13.

18. Republished as "Noticias históricas y estadísticas de la colonia y particularmente de la parte Española," transl. Carlos Curial, in Rodríguez Demorizi, op. cit., 241–289.

19. Ibid., 287–290.

20. Ibid., 270.

21. CC 9 a 45, Correspondance Interieure II, April 19, 1808. On the influence of the French Civil Code in Santo Domingo, see Cuevas Pérez and Díaz Bidó, *Presencia Francesa en Santo Domingo, 1802–1809*.

22. CC 9 a 45, Correspondance Interieure IV, August 17, 1808, Ferrand to Vicar-General Prado.

23. Ibid., CC 9 a 40, cahier 2, 3 Pluviose an 12.

24. Ibid., cahier 10, 16 Messidor an 12.

25. Ibid., CC 9 a 45, Correspondance Interieure II, May 18, 1808.

26. Ibid., May 20, 1808.

27. Ibid., CC 9 a 45, Correspondance Interieure III, June 23, 1808.

28. Ibid., cahier 14, 9 Brumaire an 13; CC 9 a 41, "Dossier concernant Mauviel [sic], évêque de Saint Domingue an XIII."

29. AN, Section Outre-Mer 5 Mi 94, "Saint-Domingue Etat Civil Santo Domingo Mariages An 10 a Vendimiaire an 14 (1801–1805)" (microfilm).

30. Ibid., 18 Pluviose an 11.

31. Ibid., Mariaes An 1806, no. 10, 17 Nivose an 14.

32. C. Lyonnet, "Estadística de la Parte Española de Santo Domingo, 1800," transl. C. Armand Rodríguez, and "resultad de la cesión de la parte española de Santo Domingo, hecha a la Francia por el Trtado de Basilea, por Don Domingo Belmonte," in Rodríguez Demorizi, op. cit., 125–126 and 42.

33. "Etat Général de la Population de la Partie de l'Est de Saint-Domingue à l'epoque du Premier Janvier 1808," CC 9 a 45.

34. Ibid.: "On en trouvera la raison dans les désastres qu'ont entouré toutes les communes frontieres de l'ancienne partie française, les plus populeuses et les plus riches, comme celles de St. Raphael, St. Michel, Hincha, Banico, Las Cahovas, La Mata, St. Jean, Neyba, de meme que Monte Christi, dans le département du Cibao.

Les familles nombreuses de ces paroisses qui ont echappée au fer des assassins revoltés ont peri presque toute par les déplorables suites du decouragement de la misere et des chagrins."

35. Ibid.: "La population se developpera surtout, et affluera plus sensiblement a Samana, par les précieux résultats de l'heureuse combinaison du commerce maritime et des cultures coloniales que la situation géographique et les nouveaux etablissements on en a fait dans cette Presqu'isle promettent d'avance a la Metropole."

36. "Etat de la culture et des animaux de toute espece de la Partie de l'Est de Saint-Domingue a l'epoque du Premier Janivier 1808," CC 9 a 45.

37. On the gradual process of transformation of the institutions of Saint Lucia, See Liverpool, *History and Development of the St. Lucia Civil Code*. On the economic development of Louisiana, see Follett, *The Sugar Masters*.

Chapter 5

1. AN, Collection Murat, 31/AP/24, Napoleon to Murat, no. 25: "Je vois que vous attachez en general trop d'importance a l'opinion de la ville de Madrid. Je n'ai pas réuni la grande armée en Espagne pour suivre les fantasies de la populace de Madrid."

2. Ibid., dossier 267: "Mon frere, je vois dans le rapport du 16 Mai du Ministre de la Marine qu'il craint que Porto Rico et la Havane ne manquent de vivres, par suite de l'embargo mis sur les batimens americains. D'abord la Havana peut s'approvisioner par la Florida et Porto Rico para le continent espagnol."

3. CC 9 a 45, "Pieces en espagnol": "Habitantes de la Isla de Cuba, Hijos Dignos de la Generosa Nación Española. Sabed que acabo de recibir hoy mismo algunos manifiestos, proclamas y bandos publicados e impresos por orden de la Junta Suprema de Gobierno que se ha establecido en Sevilla, de resultas de un acto de la perfidia mas infame que han visto ni oído los siglos."

4. Ibid.

5. Ibid.: "Españoles Puerto-Riqueños. Es demasiada savida vuestra fidelidad y lealtad a los Reyes Católicos de España desde que la Divina providencia puso esta Isla baxo su imperio, y por tanto es excusada qualquier exortacion, o Proclama para renobar en vosotros aquella leattad y fidelidad que habeis conservado, y sostenido contra los mayores ataques de los Enemigos de la Corona de España que han suspirado y suspiran sin cesar por la posesión de esta preciosa isla."

6. *Gaceta de Puerto-Rico* 3, no. 28 (August 6, 1808): "solo se oían por las calles las voces de repetidos vivas y aclamaciones y que desde la infima clase hasta la mas elevada se demostraba el gozo y alegría que había inspirado tan plausible acontecimiento. . . . El Illmo. Sr. D. Juan Alexo de Arizmendi Dignísimo Obispo de esta Diocesis arrojó en aquel día desde los balcones de su Palacio considerable cantidad de dinero al Pueblo, a impulsos del acendrado celo que ha demonstrado y observado siempre por el mayor servicio de S.m. y del singular placer de que se hallaba penetrado en aquel agradable acto."

7. CC 9 a 45, "Pieces en espagnol": "sin excepcion de persona, estado y condicion, en el Sombrero con esta diferencia, que las Milicias y empleados que disfrutan sueldo por el Rey, han de colocar en el centro de dicha cucarda, otra de color negro mas pequeña, para denotar el armisticio, y alianza entre las Naciones Española e Inglesa, y tanto estos, como los demas, podrán añadir tambien una Cifra o las Letras iniciales del Augusto nombre de Nuestro Soberano el Sr. D. Fernando VII para signficiar mas indudablemente los objetos de la insignia. Advirtiendoos que los que despues de ocho dias de la publicacion de este Edicto no la llebaren, seran tenidos por sospechosos, y se procedra contra ellos conforme a derecho."

8. CC 9 a 45, Correspondance Exterieure II, August 6, 1808: "Je ne laisserai pas ignorer au Gouvernement franèais tout l'interet que vous aurez mis a hater et a faire reussir une expédition aussi conséquentee, en la secondant de tous les moyens qui auront été a votre disposition."

9. AN, SO 5 MI 94, Marriages, Santo Domingo, no. 47.

10. CC 9 a 44, "Etat nominatif des Officiers, Sous Officiers, Soldats provenant de Santo Domingo compris dans les listes de proposition d'admission a la Légion d'Honneur . . .", Vives, "Prisionner en Angleterre."

11. CC 9 a 45, Correspondance Exterieure II, August 10, 1808: "J'avoue que je ne connais pas l'existence politique de ce Conseil, ni le caractère dont il a pu ëtre revettu pour faire des actes que appartiennent seuelement a un souverain légitime."

12. Ibid.: "que ne m'a pas paru être le signe d'aucun Gouvernement légitime et légalement reconnu." An anonymous writer in the *Gaceta de Puerto-Rico* later alleged that in this occasion Ferrand had kicked the cockade (supplement to the *Gaceta* of November 26, 1808).

13. CC 9 a 45, "Lettres du géneral Ferrand," draft of the proclamation of August 9, 1808.

14. CC 9 a 45, Correspondance Interieure IV, August 18, 1808.

15. Ibid., Correspondance Exterieure II, September 3, 1808: "Monsieur le Capitaine Générale, le ton, le stile des lettres et des proclamations dont était porteur Mr. Brasseti, m'ont fait connaitre que l'ésprit d'insurrection que regne parmi les habitans de Porto Rico, porte le même caractére et contient les mêmes élémens qui vaient conduir par degrés la révolution française, au dernier periode de barbarie et de demoralisation. J'ai été moi même temoin des tourmentes et des horreurs periodiques de cette révolution, et j'ai toujours observé que la faiblesse du gouvernement les avait en quelque sorte preparées, en ne prenant pas a temps, les mesures les plus energiques pour comprimer les mouvements, d'un peuple egarée, qui ne connait plus de frein, lorsqu'íl a fait le premier pas dans la carrière de l'anarchie et du crime et qui est pret a renverser aujourdhúi, les idoles qu'il incensait hier."

16. Ibid.: "C'est comme votre ami, comme celui des malheureux habitans de Porto-Rico, que je vous fait part de ces observations, dans lesquelles votre Excellence pourra trouver des conseils désinteresés et peutetre sages. Malheur a ceux qui provquent fomentent ou tolèrent des revolutions préparées par l'insurrection du Peuple et s'ils veulent s'éclairer par un exemple aussi instructif que terrible, qu'ils lisent et méditent les nnales effroyantes de la révolution française, qui a succesivement dévoré tous ceux qui avaient été les fauteurs de ces excèes et les partisans de ses fureurs."

17. CC 9 a 45, Correspondance Interieure IV, August 30, 1808.

18. Guillermin, *Journal historique de la Révolution de la partie de l'Est de Saint-Domingue,* 7–10.

19. Cf., e.g., the letters of Ferrand to Juan Sánchez on 17 Pluviose an 12 (CC 9 a 40, cahier 2) and 9 Vendimiaire an 13 (cahier 13).

20. PARES, Archivo Hisórico Nacional, Estado, legajo 60, expediente -41.

21. Ibid.

22. Centro de Investigaciones Históricas, Universidad de Puerto Rico, "Transcripciones del Archivo General de la Nación, México," vol. 5, taken from "Correspondencia de Gobernadores," vol. 14, 1809. On this occasion, minimizing the help received from Puerto Rico in 1808 probably reflects the deception that Sánchez Ramírez had when the new governor of Puerto Rico, Salvador Meléndez, refused in 1809 to give further help.

23. The emigrants subscribed the bond. PARES, Archivo Histórico Nacional, Junta Suprema Estado, legajo 60 C, document 48, 3 v.

24. CC 9 a 45, Correspondance a l'Interieur, cahier 5, October 10, 1808.

25. Ibid.

26. Guillermin, op. cit., 29.

27. CC 9 a 45, "Proclamation de Christophe président de l'état de Haiti."

28. PARES, Archivo Histórico Nacional, Estado, legajo 22, no. 25 C, 1 r–v. It is interesting to note that in repeated communications, Montes affirmed that he had received no answer from the Junta.

29. CC 9 a 45, Correspondance a l'Interieur, cahier 5, October 29, 1808.

30. Ibid., November 1, 1808.
31. PARES, Archivo Histórico Nacional, Estado, legajo 22, no. 357, copy of the letter which Juan Sánchez Ramírez wrote to Toribio Montes, November 9, 1808.
32. Guillermin, op. cit., 50–51.
33. Sánchez Ramírez to Montes, loc. cit. In his own report of the battle, Montes wrote that Ferrand's exhortation to his troops consisted in offering one hundred pesos to whoever captured the enemy's standard.
34. It is interesting to note that Toribio Montes, who in his report to the Junta used Sánchez Ramírez's narrative, wrote ten minutes, and that the emigrant Dominicans in theirs wrote fifteen.
35. PARES, Archivo Histórico Nacional, Junta Suprema, Estado, legajo 22, no. 359, letter from Toribio Montes to Francisco Saavedra, November 26, 1808.
36. *Gaceta de Puerto-Rico*, November 23, 1808, pp. 2150–2153.
37. Ibid., p. 2152.
38. Guillermin, op. cit.
39. PARES, Archivo Histórico Nacional, Junta Suprema, Estado, legajo 22, expediente no. 359.
40. Ibid.
41. The fiscal situation in Mexico had deteriorated. See Carlos Marichal, *La bancarrota del Virreitanto, Nueva España, y las Finanzas del Imperio Español, 1780–1810*.
42. Ibid.
43. Ibid.

Chapter 6

1. PARES, Archivo General de Indias, Estado, legajo 2, expediente 54.
2. Pérez Memén, *La Iglesia y el Estado en Santo Domingo*, 330–333.
3. CC 9 a 5, "Registre des prisonniers (civil) an XIV-1809."
4. See appendix 1.
5. See appendixes 2 and 3.
6. PARES, Archivo Histórico Nacional, Junta Suprema, Estado, legajo 22, no. 369, letter of Toribio Montes on April 6, 1809, to the secretary of state and of the office of war.
7. CC 9 a 44, "Etat nominatif des Officiers, Sous Offices, Soldats provenant de Santo Domingo compris dans les listes de proposition d'admission a la Légion d'Honneur, jointes a le depeche addressé par le M. de M. et des Col . . . a S.E. le Grand Chancellier de la Légion d'Honneur."
8. CC 9 a 44, "Etat nominatif des Officirs, Sous-Officiers et Soldats provenant de Santo Domingo proposés pour etre admis dans la Légion d'Honneur au refert desquels il a été reçu des renseignements depuis le 29 mars 1810."
9. PARES, Archivo Histórico Nacional, Estado, legajo 22, no. 363.
10. Transcripciones del Archivo General de la Nación, México, vol. 5.
11. Ibid., pp. 111–114.
12. Ibid.
13. Ibid., 105–106.
14. Ibid., 121–113, Sánchez Ramírez to the viceroy of New Spain, July 23, 1810.
15. Ibid.
16. Ibid.
17. On March 9, 1811, the governor of Puerto Rico acknowledged the receipt of a communction dated February 20, in which Manuel Caballero notified the death of Sánchez Ramírez and, as lieutenant governor, his assumption of the governorship (AGPR, FGEPR, box 34, draft of the letter).
18. Ibid.
19. AGPR, FGEPR, box 34.

Chapter 7

1. Guillermin, *Journal historique,* 55.
2. These proposals are found in CC 9 a 47. A study of their representations of what had happened in Saint-Domingue and the means of taking back the colony might be interesting.
3. Ibid., "1814 Mémoires et Lettres," "Notes sur l'Expédition de St. Domingue presentées a S.E. le Monseigneur le Ministre de la Marine et des Colonies par le Lieut. Colonel De Castel-La Boulbène."
4. At that time, Caribbean planters and the London merchants to whom they were indebted had a great deal of influence in the British Parliament. Anything that would lower European sugar prices was considered contrary to their interests. Butler, *The Economics of Emancipation.* That situation had arisen in the eighteenth century, with the dissemination of sugarcane planting in the French Caribbean. See Beckles, *A History of Barbados,* 99.
5. On the reconfiguration of French imperial ambitions from 1830 on, see Pitts, *A Turn to Empire,* 167. The author, however, does not credit the Haitian Revolution with enough impact on that process.
6. López (comp.), *La Gran Colombia y los Estados Unidos,* 2:159–160.
7. Centro de Investigaciones Históricas, Archivo General de la Nación, vol. 57, pp. 244–445, transcriptions of *Reales Cédulas,* vol. 227, expediente 2.
8. AGPR, FGEPR, box 34, letter of the governor of Santo Domingo to the governor of Puerto Rico, April 23, 1821.
9. Ibid., draft of the letter of May 17, 1821 of the governor of Puerto Rico to the governor of Santo Domingo.
10. According to Johanna von Grafenstein García, "Gregorio Mac Gregori, a Scotchman, former participant in the Bolivarian expedition issuing from Les Cayes in April of 1816, took refuge five times in Haiti. From there he departed in 1817 to found the Republic of Florida." (Grafenstein García, *Nueva España y el Circumcaribe,* 250).
11. See related documentation in Rodríguez Demorizi, *Santo Domingo y la Gran Colombia.*
12. The narration of Aybar and his companions' departure from Hispaniola is found in a letter from the mayor of Mayaguez to the governor of Puerto Rico on March 4, 1823. It was a group of twenty-nine persons "which by fortune were able to obtain exit passports" and they arrived in a pitiable state (Archivo General de Puerto Rico, Fondo de Gobernadores Españoles, box 54 [Emigrados]).

Bibliography

Manuscript Sources

Archivo General de Puerto Rico (AGPR)
Archivo Histórico Nacional (Madrid) (through PARES [Portal de Archivos Españoles])
Archives Nationales de la France (AN)
Bibliothèque Nationale de la France (BN)

Publications

The Period in General

Bukovansky, Mlada. *Legitimacy and Power Politics: The American and French Revolutions in International Political Culture.* Princeton, NJ: Princeton University Press, 2010.

Godechot, Jacques. *France and the Atlantic Revolution of the Eighteenth Century, 1770–1799.* Translated by Herbert H. Rowen. New York: Free Press, 1965.

Langley, Lester D. *The Americas in the Age of Revolution, 1750–1850.* New Haven, CT: Yale University Press, 1996.

Palmer, R. R. *The Age of the Democratic Revolution: A Political History of Europe and America, 1760–1800.* Vol. 1: *The Challenge.* Vol. : *The Struggle.* Princeton, NJ: Princeton University Press, 1959–1970.

Reed, Stephen A. *The American, French, Haitian and Spanish American Revolutions, 1775–1825: Social or Political?* 2nd ed. Dubuque, IA: Kendall Hunt, 2010.

Caribbean Countries

Association of Caribbean Historians. *Social Groups and Institutions in the History of the Caribbean: Papers Presented at the VI Annual Conference of Caribbean Historians, Puerto Rico, April 4–9, 1974.* N.p.: Association of

Caribbean Historians, 1975.

Barros, Juanita de, Audra Diptee, and David W. Trotman (eds.). *Beyond Fragmentation: Perspectives in Caribbean History.* Princeton, NJ: Markus Wiener, 2006.

Barry, Tom, Beth Wood, and Deb Preusich. *The Other Side of Paradise: Foreign Control in the Caribbean.* New York: Grove Press, 1984.

Beckles, Hilary, and Verene Shepherd. *A Caribbean Slave Society and Economy: A Student Reader.* Kingston: Ian Randle Publishers, 1991.

Beckles, Hilary McD., and Verene A. Shepherd. *Saving Souls: The Struggle to End the Transatlantic Trade in Africans: A Bicentennial Caribbean Reflection.* Kingston: Ian Randle Publishers, 2007.

Benn, Denis. *The Caribbean: An Intellectual History, 1774–2003.* Kingston: Ian Randle Publications, 2004.

Blackburn, Robin. *The Overthrow of Colonial Slavery, 1776–1848.* London: Verso, 1988.

Boutin, Raymond, Richard Cahteau-Degat, Ludie Ho-Fong Choy Choucosteau, and Georges El Mauvois. *Histoire et civilisation de la Caraibe (Guadeloupe, Martinique, Petites Antilles): La construction des sociétés antillaises des origines au temps présent: Structures et dynamiques.* Vol. 1: *Le temps des geneses, des origines a 1685.* N.p: Editions Maisonneuve et Larose, 2004.

Bruley, Georges. *Les Antilles pendant la révolution française: D'après la correspondance inédite de César Dominique Duny, consul de France a Curaçao, né a Tours le 22 juillet 1758.* Paris: Editions Caribéennes, 1989.

Buckley, Roger Norman. *The British Army in the West Indies: Society and the Military in the Revolutionary Age.* Gainesville: University Press of Florida, 1998.

Burn, W. L. *The British West Indies.* London: Hutchinson's University Library, 1951.

Cohen, David W., and Jack P. Greene. *Neither Slave nor Free: The Freedman of African Descent in the Slave Societies of the New World.* Baltimore: Johns Hopkins University Press, 1972.

Crahan, Margaret E., and Franklin Knight. *Africa and the Caribbean: The Legacies of a Link.* Baltimore and London: Johns Hopkins University Press, 1979.

Davis, David Brion. *The Problem of Slavery in the Age of Revolution, 1770–1823.* New York: Oxford University Press, 1999.

Franco, José Luciano. *Revoluciones y conflictos internacionales en el Caribe 1789–1854. La batalla por el dominio del Caribe y el Golfo de Mexico.* Havana: Instituto de Historia y Academia de Ciencias, 1965.

Francophonie et Caraibe/Francofonía y Caribe. Colloque 29 et 30 avril 1993, Maison de France [Coloquio 29 y 30 de abril de 1993, Casa de Francia. Santo Domingo: Casa de Francia, 1993.

Gall, J., and F. Gall. *El filibusterismo.* Translated by Alvaro Custodio. Mexico City: Fondo de Cultura Económica, 1957.

García Muñiz, Humberto, and Betsaida Vélez Natal. *Bibliografía militar del Caribe.* Serie bibliográfica no. 1. Río Piedras: Centro de Investigaciones Históricas, 1992.

Gaspar, Barry. *Bondsmen and Rebels.* Baltimore: Johns Hopkins University Press, 1985.

Gaspar, David Barry, and David Patrick Geggus (eds.). *A Turbulent Time: The French Revolution and the Greater Caribbean.* Bloomington: Indiana University Press, 1997.

Gautier, Arlette. *Les soeurs de solitude: La condition feminine dans l'esclave aux Antilles du XVIIe au XIXe siècle.* Paris: Éditions Caribéennes, 1985.

Geeber, Stanford N. *The Family and the Caribbean: Proceedings of the Second Conference on the Family in the Caribbean, Aruba, Netherland Antilles, December 1–5 1969.* Río Piedras: Institute of Caribbean Studies, 1973.

Goslinga, Cornelio Ch. *Los holandeses en el Caribe.* Translated by Elpidio Pacios. Havana: Casa de las Américas, 1983.

Goveia, Elsa V. *Slave Society in the British Leeward Islands at the End of the Eighteenth Century.* Institute of Caribbean Studies. New Haven, CT: Yale University Press, 1965.

Green, William A. *British Slave Emancipation, the Sugar Colonies and the Great Experiment, 1830–1865.* Oxford: Clarendon Press, 1991.

Higman, B. W. (ed.). *General History of the Caribbean.* Vol. 6: *Methodology and Historiography of the Caribbean.* London: Unesco, 1999.

Higman, B. W. (ed.). *Trade, Government and Society in Caribbean History, 1700–1920: Essays Presented to Douglas Hall.* Kingston: Heinemann Educational Books, 1983.

James, C.L.R. *Beyond a Boundary.* Introduction by Robert Lipsyte. 3rd printing. Durham: Duke University Press, 1998.

Jordan, W. F. *Crusading in the West Indies.* New York: Fleming H. Revell Company, 1922.

Kiple, Kenneth F. *The Caribbean Slave: A Biological History.* Cambridge: Cambridge University Press, 1984.

Knight, Franklin W. *The Caribbean: The Genesis of a Fragmented Nationalism.* New York: Oxford University Press, 1978.

Lafleur, Gérard. *Les Caraibes des Petites Antilles.* Paris: Editions Karthala, 1992.

Lampe, Armando (ed.). *Christianity in the Caribbean: Essays on Church History.* Kingston: University of the West Indies Press, 2001.

Lewis, Gordon K. *Main Currents in Caribbean Thought: The Historical Evolution of Caribbean in Its Ideological Aspects, 1492–1900.* Baltimore: Johns Hopkins University Press, 1983.

Look Lai, Walton. *The Chinese in the West Indies, 1806–1995: A Documentary*

History. Kingston: University of the West Indies Press, 1998.

Manning, Helen Taft. *British Colonial Government after the American Revolution, 1782–1820.* Hamden, CT: Anchor Books, 1966.

McDonald, Roderick A. (ed.). *West Indian Accounts: Essays on the History of the British Caribbean and the Atlantic Economy in Honour of Richard Sheridan.* Barbados: University of the West Indies Press, 1996.

Mintz, Sidney W. *Sweetness and Power: The Place of Sugar in Modern History.* New York: Penguin Books, 1985.

Mintz, Sidney W., and Richard Price. *The Birth of African-American Culture: An Anthropological Perspective.* Boston: Beacon Press, 1992.

Momsen, Janet H. (ed.). *Women and Change in the Caribbean: A Pan-Caribbean Perspective.* Kingston: Ian Randle Publishers, 1993.

Moore, Brian, and Swithin Wilmot (eds.). *Before and After 1865: Education, Politics and Regionalism in the Caribbean, in Honour of Sir Roger Augier.* Kingston: Ian Randle Publishers, 1998.

Mullian, Michael. *Africa in America: Slave Acculturation and Resistance in the American South and the British Caribbean, 1736–1831.* Urbana: University of Illinois Press, 1992.

Parry, J. H., and Philip Sherlock. *Historia de las Antillas.* Translated by Viviana S. de Ghis. Buenos Aires: Editorial Kapelusz, 1976.

Picó, F. "Iglesia y esclavitud en el Caribe hispano." *SIC* (Caracas) 53 (April 1990): 89–103.

Piqueras, José A. (ed.). *Las Antillas en la era de las luces y la revolución.* Madrid: Siglo XXI, 2005.

Piqueras, José A. (ed.). *Azúcar y esclavitud en el final del trabajo forzado: Homenaje a Manuel Moreno Fraginals.* Mexico City: Fondo de Cultura Económica, 2002.

Rediker, Marcus. *Between the Devil and the Deep Blue Sea: Merchant Seamen, Pirates and the Anglo-American Maritime World, 1750–1950.* Cambridge: Cambridge University Press, 1989.

Richardson, Bonham C. *Igniting the Caribbean's Past: Fire in British West Indian History.* Chapel Hill: University of North Carolina Press, 2004.

Roberts, Peter A. *From Oral to Literate Culture: Colonial Experience in the English West Indies.* Kingston: University of the West Indies Press, 1997.

Rogozinski, Jan. *A Brief History of the Caribbean: From the Arawak and the Carib to the Present.* New York: Penguin Books, 1992.

Sama-Molins, Louis. *Le code noir ou le calvaire de Canaan.* Paris: Presses Universitaires de France, 1987.

Thompson, Alvin O. *Flight to Freedom: African Runaways and Maroons in the Americas.* Kingston: University of the West Indies Press, 2006.

Thompson, Alvin O. (ed.). *In the Shadow of the Plantation: Caribbean History and Legacy. in Honour of Professor Emeritus Woodville K. Marshall.* Kingston:

Ian Randle Publishers, 2002

Toth, Charles W. *Anglo-American Diplomacy and the British West Indies, 1783–1789.* Offprint of *The Americas* 32, no. 3 (1976),

Toth, Charles W. (ed.). *The American Revolution and the West Indies.* Port Washington, NY: Kennikat Press, 1975.

United Kingdom, Parliament. *Papers Presented to the House of Commons Relating to Monsieur de Chamilly's Appointment for Raising a Corps etc. in the West Indies in 1794.* London: Parliamentary Papers, House of Commons, 1809.

Waddell, D.A.G. *The West Indies and the Guianas.* The Modern Nations in Historical Perspective. Englewood Cliffs, NJ: Prentice-Hall,1967.

Walvin, James. *Black Ivory: A History of British Slavery.* London: HarperCollins, 1992.

Williams, Eric. *Capitalism and Slavery.* New York: G. P. Putnam's Sons, 1966.

Williams, Eric. *From Columbus to Castro: The History of the Caribbean, 1492–1969.* New York: Harper & Row, 1970.

Antigua

Lowe, Robson. *The Codrington Correspondence, 1743–1851.* London: Ronson Lowe, 1951.

Lowes, Susan. *The Peculiar Class: The Formation, Collapse and Reformation of the Middle Class in Antigua, West Indies, 1834–1940.* PhD dissertation, Columbia University, 1994. Ann Arbor, MI: University Microfilms, 1994.

Bahamas

Campbell, David G. *The Ephemeral Islands: A Natural History of the Bahamas.* London: Macmillan, 1990.

Craton, Michael. *A History of the Bahamas.* 3rd ed. Waterloo, Ontario: San Salvador Press, 1990.

Craton, Michael, and Gail Saunders. *Islanders in the Stream: A History of the Bahamian People.* Vol. 1: *From Aboriginal Times to the End of Slavery.* Athens: University of Georgia Press, 1992.

Johnson, Howard. *The Bahamas from Slavery to Servitude, 1783–1933.* Gainesville: University Press of Florida, 1996.

Barbados

Beckles, Hilary. *A History of Barbados: From Amerindian Settlement to Nation State* Cambridge: Cambridge University Press, 1990.

Beckles, Hilary McD. *A History of Barbados from Amerindian Settlement to Caribbean Single Market.* Cambridge: Cambridge Univerity Press, 2006.

Handler, Jerome S. *A Guide to Source Materials for the Study of Barbados History, 1627–1834.* Carbondale: Southern Illinois University Press, 1971.

Marshall, Woodville, with Trevor Marshall and Bentley Gibbs. *The Establishment of a Peasantry in Barbados, 1840–1920*. Barbados: University of the West Indies, n.d.

Welch, Pedro L. V. *Slave Society in the City: Bridgetown, Barbados, 1680–1834*. Kingston: Ian Randle Publishers, 2004.

Bermuda

Packwood, Cyril Outerbridge. *Chained on the Rock: Slavery in Bermuda*. New York: Eliseo Torres and Sons, 1975.

Colombia

López, Luis Horacio (comp.). *La Gran Colombia y los Estados Unidos de América: Relaciones Diplomáticas, 1810–1831*. 2 volumes. Bogotá: Fundación Francisco de Paula Santander, 1990.

Cuba

Bergad, Laird W. *Cuban Rural Society in the Nineteenth Century: The Social and Economic History of Monoculture in Matanzas*. Princeton, NJ: Princeton University Press, 1990.

Bergad, Laird W., Fé Iglesias García, and María del Carmen Barcia. *The Cuban Slave Market, 1790–1880*. Cambridge: Cambridge University Press, 2003.

Franco, José Luciano. *El Gobierno Colonial de Cuba y la Independencia de Venezuela*. Estudios Monográficos Casa de las Américas 6. Havana: Casa de las Américas, 1970.

Humboldt, Alejandro de. *Ensayo político sobre la isla de Cuba*. Madrid: Ediciones Doce Calles, 1998.

Iglesias García, Fé. *Del ingenio al central*. Río Piedras: Editorial de la Universidad de Puerto Rico, 1998.

Kuette, Allan J. *Cuba, 1753–1815: Crown, Military and Society*. Knoxville: University of Tennessee Press, 1986.

La Rosa Corzo, Gabino. *Los cimarrones de Cuba*. Havana: Editorial de Ciencias Sociales, 1988.

Marrero, Levi. *Cuba: Economía y Sociedad: Azucar, Ilustración y Conciencia (1763–1868)*. 12 vols. Madrid: Editorial Playor, 1985.

Moreno Fraginals, Manuel. *El Ingenio: Complejo económico social urbano del azúcar*. 3 vols. 2nd ed. Havana: Editorial de Ciencias Sociales, 1978.

Naranjo, Consuelo (comp.). *Historia de Cuba*. Historia de las Antillas, vol. 1. Madrid: Consejo Superior de Investigaciones Científicas, 2009.

Naranjo Orovio, Consuelo, and Armando García González (eds.). *Racismo e Inmigración en Cuba en el siglo xix*. Madrid: Doce Calles, 1996.

Pérez de la Riva, Juan. *El barrcón y otros ensayos*. Havana: Editorial de Ciencias Sociales, 1975.

Pérez Guzmán, Francisco. *Bolívar y la independencia de Cuba*. Havana: Editorial Letras Cubanas, 1988.

Pérez Murillo, María Dolores. *Aspectos demográficos y sociales de la isla de Cuba en la primera mitad del siglo xix*. Cádiz: Universidad de Cádiz, 1988.

Sainz, Nicasio Silverio. *Tres vidas paralelas (F. De Arango y Parreño, Felix Varela, José A. Saco): Orígen de la nacionalidad cubana*. Miami: Ediciones Universal, 1973.

Sarracino, Rodolfo. *Inglaterra: Sus dos caras en la lucha cubana por la abolición*. Havana: Editorial Letras Cubanas, 1989.

Villaverde, Cirilo. *Diario del Rancheador*. Edited by Alberto Batista Reyes. Havana: Editorial Letras Cubanas, 1982.

Curaçao

Aizpurrua, Ramón. *Curazao y la costa de Caracas: Introducción al estudio del contrabando de la provincia de Venezuela en tiempos de la Compañia Guipuzcoana, 1730–1780*. Caracas: Academia Nacional de Historia, 1993.

Alvarez Nazario, Manuel. "El papiamento: ojeada a su pasado histórico y visión de su problemática de presente." *Atenea* (Mayaguez) 9, nos. 1–2, 9–20 (1972).

Emmanuel, Isaac Samuel. *History of the Jews of the Netherland Antilles*. Cincinnati: American Jewish Archives, 1970.

Goslinga, Cornelius Christiaan. *A Short History of the Netherlands Antilles and Surinam*. The Hague: M. Nijhoff, 1979.

Hartag, J. *Curaçao: Short History*. 3rd ed. Oranjestad, Aruba: De Wit Stores, 1973.

Dominica

Baker, Patrick L. *Centering the Periphery: Chaos, Order and the Ethnohistory of Dominica*. Kingston: University of the West Indies Press, 1994.

Borome, Joseph, et al. *Aspects of Dominican History*. Issued by the Government of Dominica to Commemorate Fifth Anniversary of Associated Statehood with Britain, November 3, 1972. Dominica: Government Printing Division, 1972.

Honychurch, Lennox. *The Dominica Story: A History of the Island*. 3rd ed. London: Macmillan Education, 1995.

Dominican Republic

Cuevas Pérez, César, and Guillermo Díaz Bidó. *Presencia Francesa en Santo Domingo, 1802–1809*. Santo Domingo: Editora Nacional, 2008.

Deive, Carlos Esteban. *Las emigraciones dominicanas a Cuba (1795–1808)*. Santo Domingo: Fundación Cultural Dominicana, 1989.

Deive, Carlos Esteban. *Los Guerrilleros Negros*. Santo Domingo: Fundación

Cultural Dominicana, 1989.

Deive, Carlos Esteban. *Tangomangos: Contrabando y piratería en Santo Domingo, 1522–1606*. Santo Domingo: Fundación Cultural Dominicana, 1996.

Guillermin, Gilbert. *Journal historique de la Révolution de la partie de l'Est de Saint-Domingue commencé le 10 aout 1808 avec une statistique sur cette partie*. Philadelphia: Imprimerie de P.M. Lafourcade, 1810.

Incháustegui, J. Merino. *Documentos para estudio: Marco del Tratado de Basilea de 1795, en la Parte Española de Santo Domingo*. Vols. 5 and 6. Buenos Aires: Academia Dominicana de la Historia, 1957.

Morales Carrión, Arturo. "El reflujo en Puerto Rico de la crisis dominico-haitiana 1791–1805." *Eme Eme* 5, no. 27 (1976).

Moreta Castillo, Américo. *La Real Audiencia de Santo Domingo (1511–1799): La Justicia en Santo Domingo de la Época Colonial*. Academia Dominicana de la Historia, vol. 88. Santo Domingo: Academia Dominicana de la Historia, 2010.

Moya Pons, Frank. *La dominación haitiana, 1822–1844*. 3rd ed. Santiago: Universidad Católica Madre y Maestra, 1978.

Peña Pérez, Frank. *Antonio Osorio: Monopolio, Contrabando y Despoblación*. Santiago: Universidad Católica Madre y Maestra, 1980.

Pérez Memém, Fernando. *La Iglesia y el Estado en Santo Domingo, 1700–1853*. 2nd ed. Santo Domingo: Secretaría de Estadosde Educación, Bellas Artes y Cultos, 1997.

Ramos, Alejandro Paulino. *Censos municipales del siglo xix y otras estadísticas de población*. Archivo General de la Nación, vol. 47. Santo Domingo: Archivo General de la Nación, 2008.

Rodríguez Demorizi, Emilio (ed.). *La Era de Francia en Santo Domingo: Contribución a su Estuiio*. Academia Dominicana de la Historia, vol. 2. Ciudad Trujillo: Editora del Caribe, 1955.

Rodríguez Demorizi, Emilio. *Santo Domingo y la Gran Colombia: Bolívar y Nuñez de Cáceres*. Academia Dominicana de la Historia, vol. 33. Santo Domingo: Editora del Caribe, 1971.

Schaeffer, Wendell G. "The Delayed Cession of Spanish Santo Domingto to France, 1795–1801." *Hispanic American Historical Review* 21 (1941): 46–68.

Grenada

Smith, M. G. *Kinship and Community in Carriacou*. New Haven, CT: Yale University Press, 1962.

Guadeloupe

Adelaide-Merlande, Jacques. *Delgrès: La Guadeloupe en 1802*. Paris: Editions Karthala, 1986.

Buffon, Alain. *Monnaie et crédit en économie coloniale: Contribution a l'histoire économique de la Guadeloupe, 1635–1919*. Bibliotheque d'histoire antillaise 8. Basse-Terre: Société d'Histoire de la Guadeloupe, 1979.

Rodigneaux, Michel. *La guerre de course en Guadeloupe XVIIIe–XIXe siècles ou Alger sous les Tropiques*. Paris: L'Harmattan, 2006.

Guyana

Thompson, Alvin. *Colonialism and Underdevelopment in Guyana, 1580–1803*. Bridgetown: Carib Research Publications, 1987.

Viotti da Costa, Emilia. *Crowns of Glory, Tears of Blood: The Demerara Slave Rebellion of 1823*. New York: Oxford University Press, 1994.

Guyana (French)

Mam-Lam-Fouck, Serge. *Histoire de la société guyanaise: Les années cruciales, 1848–1946*. Paris: Editions Caribéennes, 1987.

Haiti

Anonymous. *History of the Island of St. Domingo from Its First Discovery to the Present Period*. London: Archibald Constable & Co., 1818.

Cahier, Contenant les Plaintes, Doleances and Reclamations des Citoyens Libres and Proprietaires du Couleur de la Isle and Colonies Françaises Colons Américains. Cornell University Library Digital Collection, Ithaca, NY, n.d.

Corvington, Georges. *Port-au-Prince au cours des ans*. Vol. 1: *1743–1804: La ville coloniale et les convulsions révolutionnaries*. Montreal: Le Conseil des Arts du Canada, 2003.

Frostin, Charles. *Les revoltes blanches a Saint-Domingue aux XVII et XVIIIe siècles (Haiti avant 1789)*. Paris: L'Ecole, 1975.

Geggus, David Patrick. *Slavery, War and Revolution: The British Occupation of Saint Domingue, 1793–1798*. Oxford: Clarendon Press, 1982.

Griggs, Earl Leslie, and Clifford H. Prator (eds.). *Henry Christophe and Thomas Clarkson: A Correspondence*. New York: Greenwood Press, 1968.

Inoa, Orlando. *Bibliografía haitiana en la República Dominicana*. Serie Bibliografía Op. Cit. número no. 2. Río Piedras: Centro de Investigaciones Históricas, 1994.

Monti, Laura V. (comp.). *A Calendar of Rochambeau Papers at the University of Florida Libraries*. Gainesville: University of Florida Libraries, 1972.

Ott, Thomas O. *The Haitian Revolution, 1789–1804*. Knoxville: University of Tennessee Press, 1973.

Peyre-Ferry, Joseph Elisée. *Journal des opérations militaires de l'Armée Française a Saint-Domingue pendant les années X–XI et XII (1802 et 1803) sous les ordres des Capitaines-Géneraux Leclerc et Rochambeau*. Collection du Bicentenaire de l'Independance. Port au Prince: Editions Henri Deschamps, 2004.

Thésée, Françoise. *Négociants bordelais et colons de Saint-Domingue: Liaisons d'habitations: La maison Henry Romberg, Bapst et Cie, 1783–1793.* Paris: Société Française d'Histoire d'Outremer et Librairie Orientaliste Paul Gauthner, 1972.

Trouillot, Michel-Rolph. *Nation, State and Society in Haiti, 1804–1984.* Washington, DC: Woodrow Wilson International Center for Scholars, 1985.

Turnier, Alain. *Avec Merisier Jeannis: Une tranche de vie jacmélienne et nationale.* N.p., 1982.

Jamaica

Brathwaite, Kamau. *The Development of Creole Society in Jamaica, 1770–1820.* Introduction by B. W. Higman. Kingston: Ian Randle Publishers, 2005.

Butler, Kathleen Mary. *The Economics of Emancipation: Jamaica and Barbados, 1823–1843.* Chapel Hill: University of North Carolina Press, 1995.

Carnegie, Charles V. (ed.). *Afro-Caribbean Villages in Historical Perspective.* African-Caribbean Institute of Jamaica Research Review no. 2. Kingston: African Carribbean Institute of Jamaica, 1987.

Curtin, Philip D. *Two Jamaicas: The Role of Ideas in a Tropical Colony, 1830–1865.* New York: Atheneum, 1975.

Gordon, Shirley C. *God Almighty Made Me Free: Christianity in Preemancipation Jamaica.* Bloomington: Indiana University Press, 1996.

Gordon, Shirley C. *Our Cause for His Glory: Christianization and Emancipation in Jamaica.* Kingston: University of the West Indies Press, 1998.

Hall, Douglas. *Free Jamaica, 1838–1865: An Economic History.* New Haven, CT: Yale University Press, 1959.

Hall, Douglas. *Planters, Farmers and Gardeners in Eighteenth Century Jamaica.* The 1987 Elsa Goveia Memorial Lecture. Kingston: Department of History, University of the West Indies at Mona, 1988.

Hall, Neville A. T. "Public Office and Private Gain: A Note on Administration in Jamaica in the Later Eighteenth Century." *Caribbean Studies* 12, no. 3 (1972): 5–20.

Higman, B. W. *Jamaica Surveyed: Plantation Maps and Plans of the Eighteenth and Nineteenth Centuries.* Kingston: Institute of Jamaica Publications, 1989.

Higman, B. W. *Slave Population and Economy in Jamaica, 1807–1834.* Barbados: University of the West Indies Press, 1995.

Higman, B. W. *Montpelier, Jamaica: A Plantation Community in Slavery and Freedom 1739–1912.* With contributions by George A. Aarons, Karlis Karklins, and Elizabeth J. Reitz. Kingston: University of the West Indies Press, 1998.

Holt, Thomas C. *The Problem of Freedom: Race, Labor and Politics in Jamaica and Britain, 1832–1938.* Baltimore: Johns Hopkins University Press, 1992.

Ingram, K. E. *Manuscript Sources for the History of the West Indies with Special Reference to Jamaica in the National Library of Jamaica and Supplementary*

Sources in the West Indies, North America, the United Kingdom and Elsewhere. Kingston: University of the West Indies Press, 2000.

Mair, Lucille Mathurin. *Women Field Workers in Jamaica During Slavery.* The 1986 Elsa Goveia Memorial Lecture. Kingston: Department of History, University of the West Indies at Mona, 1987.

McDonald, Roderick A. *The Economy and Material Culture of Slaves: Goods and Chattels on the Sugar Plantations of Jamaica and Louisiana.* Baton Rouge: Louisiana State University Press, 1993.

Osborne, Francis H., S.J. *History of the Catholic Church in Jamaica.* 2nd ed. Chicago: Loyola University Press, 1988.

Patterson, Orlando. *The Sociology of Slavery: An Analysis of the Origins, Development and Structue of Negro Slave Society in Jamaica.* Jamaica: Sangster's Book Stores, 1973.

Sherlock, Philip, and Hazel Bennett. *The Story of the Jamaican People.* Kingston: Ian Randle; Princeton, NJ: Markus Wiener, 1998.

Stewart, Robert J. *Religion and Society in Post-Emancipation Jamaica.* Knoxville: University of Tennessee Press, 1992.

Marie Galante

Bogat, David. "Marie-Galante Colonie Indépendante sous la Révolution." *Revue Guadeloupénne* new series, no. 13 (1947): 9–23.

Martinique

Archives Départementales de la Martinique. *L'habitation, domain terrier des Antilles avant et apres la Revolution Industrielle: Edition de textes.* Fort de France: Centre Régional de Documentation Pédagogique, 1984.

Archives Départementales de la Martinique. *La Martinique pendant la Révolution de 1789: Edition de textes.* Fort de France: Le Centre Départemental de Documentation Pédagogique, 1977.

Bureau du Patrimonie du Conseil Régional de la Martinique. *Usines et habitations-sucreries: Trois siècles de patrimonie industriel martiniquais.* Fort de France: Conseil Régional de la Martinique, 1987.

Celma, Cecile. *Guide des sources disponibles sur la Revolution de St Domingue en Guadeloupe, Guyane, Haiti, Martinique.* Fort de France: Association des Archivistes, Bibliothecaiures Documentalistes Francophones de la Caraibe, n.d.

Delisle, Philippe. *Renouveau missionaire et société esclavagiste: La Martinique, 1815–1848.* N.p.: Publisud, 1997.

Forster, Elborg, and Robert Forster (eds.). *Sugar and Slavery, Family and Race: The Letters and Diaries of Pierre Dessalles, Planter in Martinique, 1808–1856.* Baltimore: Johns Hopkins University Press, 1996.

Horowitz, Michael M. *Morne-Paysan: Peasant Village in Martinique.* Case

Studies in Cultural Anthropology. New York. Holt, Rinehart and Winston, 1967.

Lémery, Henry. *La Révolution Française a la Martinique*. Paris: Larose, 1936.

Price, Richard. *The Convict and the Colonel*. Boston: Beacon Press, 1998.

Rosélie, Roland, and Elyane Jean-Louis. *L'habitation sucrière au quartier La Dumaine Le Francois*. N.p.: Foyer Rural de Dumaine et de la Cooperative Scolaire de Dumaine, 1986.

Schloss, Rebecca Hartkofp. "The February 1831 Slave Uprising in Martinique and the Policing of White Identity." *French Historical Studies* 30 (2007): 203–236.

Thesee, Françoise. *Les Ibos de l'Amelie: Destinée d'une cargaison de traite clandestine à la Martinique, 1822–1838*. Paris: Editions Caribéennes, 1986.

Tomich, Dale W. *Slavery in the Circuit of Sugar: Martinique and the World Economy, 1830–1848*. Baltimore: Johns Hopkins University Press, 1990.

Mexico

Grafenstein García, Johanna von. *Nueva España en el Circuncaribe, 1779–1808: Revolución, Competencia Imperial y Vínculos Internacionales*. Mexico City: Universidad Nacional Autonoma de Mexico, 1997.

Marichal, Carlos. *La bancarrota del Virreinato, Nueva España, y las Finanzas del Imperio Español, 1780–1810*. México: El Colegio de México y Fondo de Cultura Económica, 1999.

Transcripciones del Archivo General de la Nación, México, vol. 5. In *Correspondencia de Gobernadores*, vol. 14 (1809). Centro de Investigaciones Históricas, Universidad de Puerto Rico.

Montserrat

Akenson, Donald Harman. *If the Irish Ran the World: Montserrat 1630–1730*. Montreal: McGill-Queen's University Press, 1997.

Puerto Rico

Beale, Robert. *A Report of the Trial of Commodore David Porter of the Navy of the United States Before a General Court Martial Held at Washington, in July 1825: A Review of the Court's Decision*. Washington, DC: n.p. 1825.

Chinea, Jorge Luis. *Race and Labor in the Hispanic Caribbean: The West Indian Immigrant Worker Experience in Puerto Rico, 1800–1850*. Gainesville: University Press of Florida, 2005.

Córdoba, Pedro Tomás de. *Memoria sobre todos los ramos de la administración de la Isla de Puerto Rico*. 2nd ed. San Juan: Academica Puertorriqueña de la Historia, 2001.

Flinter, George. *An Account of the Present State of the Island of Puerto Rico*. Facsimile ed. San Juan: Academia Puertorriqueña de la Historia, 2002.

López Cantos, Angel. *Miguel Enríquez, Corsario Boricua del siglo XVIII*. San Juan: Ediciones Puerto, 1994.

Marazzi, Rosa. *El impacto de la inmigración a Puerto Rico 1800–1830: Análisis estadístico*. Río Piedras: Centro de Investigaciones Sociales, Universidad de Puerto Rico, 1975.

Navarro García, Jesús Raúl. *Puerto Rico a la sombra de la independencia continental, 1815–1840*. Seville: Escuela de Estudios Hispanoamericanos; San Juan: Centro de Estudios Avanzados de Puerto Rico y el Caribe, 1999.

Pacheco Díaz, Angélica. *Una estrategia imperial: El situado de Nueva España a Puerto Rico, 1765–1821*. México: Instituto Mora, 2005.

Proceedings of the Court of Inquiry and Court Martial in Relation to Commodore Porter. Offprint of *Gales and Seaton's Register of Debates in Congress* (December 1825), pp. 25, 56–66 (Senate); and 806–808 and 815 (House).

Rivera, Antonio (comp.). *Circulares de Don Toribio Montes*. Typewritten transcription (1949) at the Colección Puertorriqueña, Biblioteca General, Universidad de Puerto Rico, Río Piedras.

Rosario Rivera, Raquel. *Los emigrantes llegados a Puerto Rico procdentes de Venezuela entre 1810–1848 (Incluye Registro de Emigrados)*. Hato Rey: privately printed, 1992.

Zapatero, Juan Manuel. *La guerra del Caribe en el siglo xviii*. San Juan: Instituto de Cultura Puertorriqueña, 1964.

Saint Bartholomew

Lavoie, Yolande, Francine Mayer, and Carolyn Flick. "A Particular Study of Slavery in the Caribbean Island of Saint-Barthelemy, 1648–1846." *Caribbean Studies* 28, no. 2 (1993): 369–403.

Saint Eustatius

Aceto, Michael. "Statian Creole English: An English-Derived Language Emerges in the Dutch Antilles." *World Englishes* 25, nos. 3–4 (August–November 2006): 411–435.

Saint Kitts and Nevis

Cox, Edward. *Free Coloreds in the Slave Societies of St. Kitts and Grenada, 1763–1833*. Knoxville: University of Tennessee Press, 1984.

Merrill, Gordon C. *The Historical Geography of St. Kitts and Nevis, The West Indies*. Mexico City: Instituto Panamericano de Geografía e Historia, 1958.

Saint Lucia

Barrow, Christine. *Family, Land and Development in St. Lucia*. Cave Hill, Barbados: University of the West Indies, 1992.

Easter, B. H. *St. Lucia and the French Revolution*. Tom Ferguson Memorial

Lecture, 1965. Castries: n.p., 1965.

Lasalle de Louisenthal, Guillaume Albert. *Aventures de guerre aux Antilles: Sainte-Lucie, la Martinique, Trinidad, 1796–1805*. Edited by G. Debien. La Roche sur Yon: Imprimerie Centinele de l'Ouest, 1980.

Liverpool, Nicholas Joseph Orville. *The History and Development of the St. Lucia Civil Code*. Cave Hill, Barbados: Institute of Social and Economic Research, 1977.

Saint Vincent

Duncan, Ebenezer. *A Brief History of Saint Vincent, with Studies in Citizenship*. 3rd ed. Kingstown, St. Vincent: privately printed, 1963.

Price, Neil. *Behind the Planter's Back: Lower Class Responses to Marginality in Bequis Island, St. Vincent*. Warwock University Caribbean Studies. London: Macmillan, 1988.

Surinam

Price, Richard. *First Time: The Historical Vision of an Afro-American People*. Baltimore: Johns Hopkins University Press, 1983.

Price, Richard. *Saramaka Social Structure: Analysis of a Maroon Society in Surinam*. Caribbean Monographs Series no. 12. Río Piedras: Institute of Caribbean Studies, 1975.

Tobago

Keith, Keuk O. *Tobago in Wartine 1793–1815*. Kingston: University of the West Indies Press, 1995.

Trinidad

Brereton, Bridget. *Law, Justice and Empire: The Colonial Career of John Gorrie, 1829–1892*. Kingston: University of the West Indies Press, 1992.

Brown, Deryck R. *History of Money and Banking in Trinidad and Tobago from 1789 to 1989*. Edited by Terence W. Farrell and Penelope Forde. Port of Spain: Central Bank of Trinidad and Tobago, 1989.

Campbell, Carl C. *Cedulants and Capitulants: The Politics of the Coloured Opposition in the Slave Society of Trinidad, 1783–1838*. Port of Spain: Paria Publishing Co., 1992.

Higman, B. W. "The Chinese in Trinidad, 1806–1838." *Caribbean Studies* 12, no. 3 (1972): 21–44.

Liverpool, Hollis "Chalkdust." *Rituals of Power and Rebellion: The Carnival Tradition in Trinidad and Tobago, 1763–1962*. Chicago: Research Associates Publications, 2001.

Millette, James. *El sistema colonial inglés en Trinidad (1783–1810)*. Havana: Casa de las Américas, 1985.

Trotman, David Vicent. *Crime in Trinidad: Conflict and Control in a Plantation Society, 1838–1900*. Knoxville: University of Tennessee Press, 1986.

Verteuil, Anthony de, C. S. Sp. *Begorrat Brunton: A History of Diego Martin, 1784–1884*. Port of Spain: Paria Publishing Co., 1987.

Venezuela

Arcaya, Pedro M. *Insurrección de los Negros de la Serranía de Coro*. Caracas: Instituto Panamericano de Geografía e Historia, 1949.

Izard, Michel, et al. *Política y economía en Venezuela 1810–1991*. Caracas: Fundación John Boulton, 1992.

Izard, Miguel. *Tierra Firme: Historia de Venezuela y Colombia*. Madrid: Alianza Editorial, 1987.

Mayo, Lila, de Chápite, and José J. Hernández Palomo. *El cabildo de Caracas (1750–1821)*. Seville: Consejo Superior de Investigaciones Científicas y Cabildo Metropolitano de Caracas, 2002.

Páez, José Antonio. *Autobiografía del General José Antonio Páez*. 2 vols. Caracas: Academia Nacional de la Historia, 1973.

Virgin Islands (British)

Harrigan, Norwell, and Pearl Varlock. *The British Virgin Islands (A Chronology)*. Tortola: Research and Consulting Services, 1970.

Virgin Islands (Danish)

Gobel, Erik. *A Guide to Sources for the History of the Danish West Indies (U.S. Virgin Islands), 1671–1917*. Odense: University Press of Southern Denmark, 2002.

Hall, Neville A. T. *The Danish West Indies: Empire without Dominion, 1671–1848*. Occasional Paper no. 8. U.S. Virgin Islands: Division of Libraries, Museums and Archaeological Services, 1985.

Oldendorp, C.O.A. *History of the Mission of the Evangelical Brethren on the Caribbean Islands of St. Thomas, St. Croix and St. John*. Edited by Johan Jakob Bossard. Translated by Arnold R. Highfield and Vladimir Barac. Ann Arbor, MI: Karoma Publishers, 1987.

Varlock, Pearl, and Norwell Harrigan. *The Virgins: A Descriptive and Historical Profile*. Saint Thomas: Caribbean Research Institute, College of the Virgin Islands, 1971.

Other Countries Linked to the Caribbean in This Period

Argentina

Cordery, Lindsey, and Beatriz Vegh (eds.). *Melville, Conrad: Imaginarios y Américas: Reflexiones desde Montevideo*. Montevideo: Linardi y Risso, 2006.

Brazil

Haring, C. H. *Empire in Brazil: A New World Experiment with Monarchy.* Cambridge, MA: Harvard University Press, 1958.

France

Bizardel, Yvon. *Les américains a Paris pendant la Révolution.* Paris: Calmann-Lévy, 1972.

Bonaparte, Napoléon. *Correspondance générale.* Vol. 3: *Pacifications, 1800–1802.* Edited by Thierry Lentz and Gabriel Masdec. Paris: Librairie Artheme Fayard, 2006.

Bonaparte, Napoléon. *Correspondance générale.* Vol. 4: *Ruptures et fondation, 1803–1804.* Edited by François Hordeck y Gabriel Masdec. Paris: Librairie Artheme Fayard, 2003.

Bonaparte, Napoléon. *Correspondance générale.* Vol. 6: *Vers ke Grand Empire, 1806.* Paris: Librairie Antheme Fayard, 2008.

Bosher, J. F. *French Finances, 1770–1795: From Business to Bureaucracy.* Cambridge: Cambridge University Press, 2008.

Bosher, J. F. *The French Revolution.* New York: W.W. Norton and Company, 1988.

Boulle, Pierre H. *Race et esclavage dans la France de l'Ancien Régime.* N.p.: Perrin, 2007.

Cobb, Richard. *Les armées révolutionnaires: Instrument de la Terreur dans les départements. Avril 1793–Floréal An II.* 2 vols. Paris: Mouton & Co., 1961.

Cobban, Alfred. *The Social Interpretation of the French Revolution.* Cambridge: Cambridge University Press, 1964.

Cottias, Myriam, and Arlette Farge (eds.). *De la necessité d'adopter l'esclavage en France.* Paris: Bayard, 2007.

Ehrard, Jean. *Lumières et Esclavage: L'esclavage colonial et l'opinion publique en France au XVIIIe siècle.* Paris: André Versaille, Editeur, 2008.

Fonville, Robert. *Un général jacobin de la Révolution et de l'Empire: Claud Ignace François Michaud.* Annales Litteraires de l'Université de Besançon, no. 214. Paris: Les Belles Lettres, 1978.

Grégoire, Henri. *De la traite et de l'esclavage des noirs.* Preface by Aimé Césaire. Paris: Arlier, 2007.

Grégoire, Henri. *On the Cultural Achievements of Negroes.* Translated by Thomas Cassirer and Jean-François Briére. Amherst: University of Massachussets Press, 1996.

Moisy, Claude. *Le citoyen Genet: La Révolution française a l'assaunt de l'Amérique.* Paris: Editions Privat, 2007.

Moreau de St. Méry's American Journey [1793–1798]. Translated and edited by Kenneth Roberts and Anna M. Roberts. Garden City, NY: Doubleday &

Company, 1947.

Nelson, William Max. "Making Men: Enlightenment Ideas of Racial Engineering." *American Historical Review* 115, no. 5 (December 2010): 364–394.

Pitts, Jennifer. *A Turn to Empire: The Rise of Imperial Liberalism in Britain and France*. Princeton: Princeton University Press, 2003.

Régent, Frédéric. *La France et ses esclaves: De la colonisation aux abolitions (1620–1848)*. Paris: Bernard Grasset, 2002.

Sala-Molins, Louis. *Le Code Noir ou la Calvaire de Canaan*. Paris: Presses Universitaires de France, 1987.

Scott, Samuel T. *From Yorktown to Valmy: The Transformation of the French Army in the Age of Revolution*. Niwot: University of Colorado Press, 1998.

Whitridge, Arnold. *Rochambeau*. New York: Collier Books, 1965

Great Britain

Namier, Lewis. *England in the Age of the American Revolution*. 2nd ed. New York: St. Martin's Press, 1966.

United Kingdom, Parliament. *Papers Presented to the House of Commons Relating to Monsieur de Chamilly's Appointment for Raising a Corps etc. in the West Indies in 1794*. London: Parliamentary Papers, House of Commons, 1809.

White, Colin, and the 1805 Club. *The Trafalgar Captains: Their Lives and Memorials*. Annapolis: Naval Institute Press, 2005.

United States

Blanchard, Claude. *The Journal of Claude Blanchard, Commissary of the French Auxiliary Army Sent to the United States during the American Revolution, 1780–1783*. Lightning Source, UK; Milton Keynes, 2010.

Bonsal, Stephen. *When the French Were Here: A Narrative of the Sojourn of the French Forces in America and Their Contribuiton to the Yorktown Campaign Drawn from Unpublished Reports and Letters of Participants in the National Archives of France and the MS Division of the Libary of Congress*. Garden City, NY: Doubleday, Doran and Company, 1945.

Bumsted, J. M. (ed.). *The Great Awakening: The Beginning of Evangelical Pietism in America*. Waltham, MA: Blaisdell Publishing Company, 1970.

Chastellux, Marquis de. *Travels in North America in the Years 1780, 1781, and 1782*. 2 vols.Translated by Howard C. Price Jr. Chapel Hill: University of North Carolina Press, 1963.

Follett, Richard. *The Sugar Masters: Planters and Slaves on Louisiana's Cane World, 1820–1860*. Baton Rouge: Louisiana State University Press, 2005

Fruchtman, Jack, Jr. *Atlantic Cousins: Benjamin Franklin and His Visionary Friends*. New York: Thunder's Mouth Press, 2005.

Grasso, Christopher. *A Speaking Aristocracy: Transforming Public Discourse in*

Eighteenth-Century Connecticut. Chapel Hill: University of North Carolina Press, 1999.

Journal of the Siege of York-Town: Unpublished Journal of the Siege of York-town in 1781 Operated by the General Staff of the French Army, as Recorded in the Hand of Gaspard de Gallatin and translated by the French Department of the College of William and Mary. 71st Cong., 3d Sess., S. Doc. 322. Washington, DC: Government Printing Office, 1931.

Miranda, Francisco de. *The New Democracy in America: Travels of Francisco de Miranda in the United States, 1783–1784*. Translated by Judson P. Wood. Edited by John S. Ezell. Norman: University of Oklahoma Press, 1963.

Morgan, William James. *"The Pivot Upon Which Everything Turned": French Naval Superiority That Ensured Victory at Yorktown*. Washington, DC: Naval Historical Foundation, 1981.

Patton, Robert H. *Patriot Pirates: The Privateer War for Freedom and Fortune in the American Revolution*. New York: Pantheon Books, 2008.

Rahove, Jack. *Revolutionaries: A New History of the Invention of America*. Boston: Houghton Mifflin Harcourt, 2010.

Schama, Simon. *Rough Crossings: Britain, the Slaves and the American Revolution*. New York: HarperCollins, 2006.

Schechter, Barnet. *The Battle for New York: The City at the Heart of the American Revolution*. New York: Penguin Books, 2002.

Toth, Charles W. (ed.). *The American Revolution and the West Indies*. Port Washington, NY: Kennikat Press, 1975.

Unger, Harlow Giles. *John Hancock: Merchant King and American Patriot*. Edison, NJ: Castle Books, 2005.

Related Books by Markus Wiener Publishers

CARIBBEAN

1959: The Year That Inflamed the Caribbean by Bernard Diederich
A historically compelling book.
HC ISBN 978-1-55876-491-0   PB ISBN 978-1-55876-492-7

Caribbean: Sea of the New World by Germán Arciniegas
"A whacking good story." —*San Francisco Chronicle*
PB ISBN 978-1-55876-312-8

The Chinese in the Caribbean edited by Andrew Wilson
"Well documented . . . artfully balanced." —*Caribbean Studies Journal*
HC ISBN 978-1-55876-314-2   PB ISBN 978-1-55876-315-9

***Frontiers, Plantations, and Walled Cities: Essays on Society, Culture, and
Politics in the Hispanic Caribbean, 1800-1945*** by Luis Martínez-Fernández
HC ISBN 978-1-55876-511-5   PB ISBN 978-1-55876-512-2

History of the Caribbean by Frank Moya Pons
The latest book by this leading historian.
HC ISBN 978-1-55876-414-9   PB ISBN 978-1-55876-415-6

Once Jews: Stories of Caribbean Sephardim by Josette Capriles Goldish
The story of the families who can trace their ancestry back
to the early Sephardim of the Dutch island of Curaçao.
HC ISBN 978-1-55876-493-4   PB ISBN 978-1-55876-494-1

***One Frenchman, Four Revolutions: General Ferrand and the
Peoples of the Caribbean*** by Fernando Picó
HC ISBN 978-1-55876-539-9   PB ISBN 978-1-55876-540-5

Space and History in the Caribbean by Oruno D. Lara
"Superbly written and ably presented." —*Midwest Book Review*
HC ISBN 978-1-55876-400-2   PB ISBN 978-1-55876-401-9

CUBA

Afro-Cuban Myths: Yamayá and Other Orishas by Rómulo Lachatañeré
"Exciting to read, and thought provoking." —*Midwest Book Review*
HC ISBN 978-1-55876-317-3   PB ISBN 978-1-55876-318-0

Afro-Cuban Religions by Miguel Barnet
"Illuminates the complex pantheon of deities worshipped
in each tradition." —*Library Journal*
HC ISBN 978-1-55876-254-1   PB ISBN 978-1-55876-255-8

Cuban Music by Maya Roy
"Indispensable." —*Percussions*
HC ISBN 978-1-55876-281-7   PB ISBN 978-1-55876-282-4

The Island of Cuba by Alexander von Humboldt
Winner of the *Lydia Cabrera Award.*
HC ISBN 978-1-55876-242-8   PB ISBN 978-1-55876-243-5

Tropical Diaspora: The Jewish Experience in Cuba by Robert M. Levine
PB ISBN 978-1-55876-521-4

DOMINICAN REPUBLIC

Dominican Cultures: The Making of a Caribbean Society
edited by Bernardo Vega
"[A] fine collection of essays." —*Hispanic American Historical Review*
HC ISBN 978-1-55876-434-7   PB ISBN 978-1-55876-435-4

The Dominican People: A Documentary History
edited by Ernesto Sagás and Orlando Inoa
"Concise and satisfying . . . solid and convincing."
—*Hispanic American Historical Review*
HC ISBN 978-1-55876-296-1   PB ISBN 978-1-55876-297-8

The Dominican Republic: A National History by Frank Moya Pons
"Agreeable and clearly written . . . an indispensable reference."
—*Hispanic American Historical Review*
HC ISBN 978-1-55876-191-9   PB ISBN 978-1-55876-192-6

*The Impact of Intervention: The Dominican Republic During
the U.S. Occupation of 1916-1924* by Bruce J. Calder
"A comprehensive and tolerant study, devoid of jargon."
—*New York Times Book Review*
PB ISBN 978-1-55876-386-9

Trujillo: The Death of the Dictator by Bernard Diederich
"Superb. . . . A painstaking documentary thriller." —*New Society*
PB ISBN 978-1-55876-206-0

HAITI

Bon Papa: Haiti's Golden Years by Bernard Diederich
A history of the beautiful bygone Haiti whose future was full of promise.
HC ISBN 978-1-55876-464-4   PB ISBN 978-1-55876-465-1

Libète: A Haiti Anthology edited by Charles Arthur and Michael Dash
"Indispensable." —*French Review*
PB ISBN 978-1-55876-230-5

Life in a Haitian Valley by Melville J. Herskovits
"The best book on Haiti." —*Books*
PB ISBN 978-1-55876-455-2

***The Murderers among Us: History of Repression and Rebellion in Haiti
under Dr. François Duvalier, 1962-1971*** by Bernard Diederich
HC ISBN 978-1-55876-541-2   PB ISBN 978-1-55876-542-9

Papa Doc and the Tonton Macoutes by Bernard Diederich and Al Burt
"A very full account of Duvalier's reign which will be indispensable to
future historians." —Graham Greene, from the Foreword
PB ISBN 978-1-55876-290-9

***The Price of Blood: History of Repression and Rebellion in Haiti under
Dr. François Duvalier, 1957-1961*** by Bernard Diederich
HC ISBN 978-1-55876-528-3   PB ISBN 978-1-55876-529-0

JAMAICA

Black Rebels: African-Caribbean Freedom Fighters in Jamaica
by Werner Zips
"[A] stimulating and well researched study." —*New West Indian Guide*
HC ISBN 978-1-55876-212-1   PB ISBN 978-1-55876-213-8

The Story of the Jamaican People by Philip Sherlock and Hazel Bennett
"Inspiring and accessible telling of Jamaican history . . .
a significant contribution." —*New West Indian Guide*
PB ISBN 978-1-55876-146-9

NICARAGUA

Somoza and the Legacy of U.S. Involvement in Central America
by Bernard Diederich
"[A] perceptive, carefully documented, and readable account."
—*Business Week*
PB ISBN 978-1-55876-411-8

PUERTO RICO

American Colonialism in Puerto Rico by Efrén Rivera Ramos
"Provocative, extremely well documented, and innovative." —*El Nuevo Día*
PB ISBN 978-1-55876-410-1

Battleship Vieques: Puerto Rico from World War II to the Korean War
by César Ayala Casás and José Bolívar Fresneda
HC ISBN 978-1-55876-537-5 PB ISBN 978-1-55876-538-2

Clemente! The Enduring Legacy by Kal Wagenheim
PB ISBN 978-1-55876-527-6

Cuentos: Stories from Puerto Rico compiled and edited by Kal Wagenheim
A bilingual anthology of "stories . . . told by writers of acute perception
and strong powers of invention." —*Library Journal*
PB ISBN 978-1-55876-478-1

History of Puerto Rico: A Panorama of Its People by Fernando Picó
Outstanding Academic Title of the Year. "Excellent . . .
inordinately rich." —*Choice*
HC ISBN 978-1-55876-370-8 PB ISBN 978-1-55876-371-5

*A New Deal for the Tropics: Puerto Rico during the
Depression Era, 1932-1935* by Manuel R. Rodríguez
HC ISBN 978-1-55876-517-7 PB ISBN 978-1-55876-518-4

The Pond [La Charca: Puerto Rico's 19th-Century Masterpiece]
by Manuel Zeno-Gandía
"The first English translation of a classic of Latin American fiction . . .
depicting life in [19th-century] Puerto Rico." —*The Nation*
PB ISBN 978-1-55876-092-9

The Puerto Ricans: A Documentary History
Edited by Kal Wagenheim and Olga Jiménez de Wagenheim
"An essential source book for a better understanding of the
Puerto Ricans." —*The New York Times*
PB ISBN 978-1-55876-476-7

Puerto Rico: An Interpretive History from Pre-Columbian Times to 1900
by Olga Jiménez de Wagenheim
"A work of substantive scholarship and meticulous research."
—*Midwest Book Review*
HC ISBN 978-1-55876-121-6 PB ISBN 978-1-55876-122-3